Dear J

God

Thank you for all you did to help the children we served. Love,

Don Thompson

Psalm 23

Daily Praise Moments:

Gaining Strength for Today's Challenges

Volume 1 – January thru March

Dr. Don Thompson

Every attempt has been made to credit the sources of copyrighted material used in this book. If any such acknowledgement as been inadvertently omitted or miscredited, receipt of such information would be appreciated.

Special thanks to Performance Press
Printed by CreateSpace, Inc.

ISBN: 978-0-942442-80-9

First Printing 12-2017
Manufactured in the United States of America
Author email: donthompsondpm@gmail.com

Dedicated to Thomas John McKay, Sr.

My Dear Friend, Spiritual Brother, Confidant and Encourager

A True Soldier of the Cross

About the Author

Don Thompson has been immersed in church from the time he was first knit together in his mother's womb! Scripture and songs are both important to him. In fact, he often answers questions by singing or quoting song lyrics!

Though you may not know it from interacting with him, Don has faced major health challenges in his life, but he is quick to tell you that these hardships strengthened his faith in God and gave him compassion for helping others.

Don began his professional career as a sociology instructor at Maryville College. He changed careers after one year and began serving children with disabilities. In 1972, he became a Vocational Rehabilitation Counselor serving students at the Tennessee School for the Deaf. In 1976, he became the director of the Comprehensive Educational Resource Center at TSD. In this role, he helped establish the West Tennessee School for the Deaf in Jackson, TN. One of the programs he supervised was a home-based early intervention program helping families whose young children have major developmental challenges. Under his leadership, this program grew from one full-time teacher to 37 full-time and 600 part-time teachers before it was merged into another state program. Don now serves as Volunteer Executive Director of Friends of Tennessee's Babies with Special Needs, a non-profit he helped establish twenty-one years ago.

God satisfied Don's musical interests through his church, Everett Hills Baptist, in Maryville, Tennessee, where he served as part-time music director for more than 20 years.

Don holds a doctorate in Educational Leadership from the University of Tennessee, with an emphasis in home-based early childhood special education.

Don and his lovely wife, Janet, have been married for 48 years and have two fine sons, two wonderful daughters-in-law, and two outstanding granddaughters! Just enter into conversation with him, and he will proudly tell you all about each of them!

Acknowledgements

Hebrews 10:23-25 (NASB) says:
23 Let us hold fast the confession of our hope without wavering, for He
who promised is faithful; 24 and let us consider how to stimulate one
another to love and good deeds, 25 not forsaking our own assembling
together, as is the habit of some, but encouraging one another; and all
the more as you see the day drawing near.

Many folks have encouraged me on to compile my Daily Praise Moments into a book. At the risk of overlooking significant encouragers, I'd like to express deep appreciation to some of the many friends who cheered me on.

Linda Albert gave me encouragement and feedback as she read drafts and offered suggestions. In the process, we've become dear friends, so Linda, "thank you!"

To Dr. Larry Perry, I say "thank you" for meeting with me and giving me feedback. Also, I greatly appreciate how you modeled positive, godly interaction with restaurant staff as we met for lunch on numerous occasions. You were always the encourager, helping each person state their dream and begin putting actions to their desires to achieve at a higher level, look higher than they were looking, coaching them to set goals and start the journey to reach upward.

To Janet, my precious wife of forty-eight years, I say "THANK YOU" for your encouraging remarks and for living through the extreme clutter that, for reasons I don't understand, must be my preferred writing environment. I love you, Babe!

To Rev. Armond Whitehurst, a dear friend who encouraged me, prayed with me, posted my Daily Praise Moments on his Facebook page and gave me permission to use content from two of his sermons in my DPMs, I say, "Thank you, man of God."

To Delight Everett, my dear friend, I say "thank you" for reading my DPMs, sharing them with friends and inviting Janet and me to your home to meet one of your dear friends whose personal story is recorded in Daily Praise Moments.

Thank you, Bob Woodworth, for being brave enough to tell me to do a fact check on some of my content before putting it in print. Bob, I love you and appreciate your friendship and feedback.

Special thanks to my son, Dan, for taking the images and designing the covers of the four volumes in this set.

Special thanks to family and friends who suffered through reading about themselves in some of the snippets I've included in Daily Praise Moments.

Though my Mom and Dad are home in heaven, I am eternally grateful for the spiritual heritage they gave me through their unconditional love and example.

Most important of all, I say THANK YOU to my Lord and Savior, Jesus Christ, for loving me, adopting me into Your family and meeting my needs each moment of my life. Without You, I am nothing, but as the Apostle Paul wrote in Philippians 4:18, with You, I "have all and abound"….

Foreword

Daily Praise Moments was written for you!

When I began writing Daily Praise Moments, my desire was to help believers focus on how Almighty God loves them and walks with them every step of life's way.

My motive in publishing this book is to fan the flames of praise in believers' hearts. As we get a clearer, more comprehensive picture of how Jesus Christ meets our daily needs, our praise for Him grows. The more we see His all-encompassing love and provision for us, the more we trust Him with every detail of our lives. And, the more we trust Him, the more we are willing to listen to His voice and follow His will for our lives.

Begin each day praising God and stand in awe of how God miraculously uses you to make a difference in your family, your community and your world.

My prayers are with you as you lift praises to our soon-coming Savior, the Lord Jesus Christ.

Shalom!

Don

Don Thompson, Ed. D.

Daily Praise Moment

January 1

Praising Almighty God on Day One of the New Year

What better way to start the New Year than with Genesis 1:1 (NIV) which says:
In the beginning, God (ELOHIM) created the heavens and the earth.

God brought us safely through the past year, and He is leading us into the new year. And, praise the Lord, He is still in control.

Thinking about Creator God leads me to pray these words:
Creator God, You made the heavens and the earth. All things were made by You and for You, including me.

Psalm 139:16 (NIV) shows your ownership and direction over my life:
Your eyes saw my unformed body; all the days ordained for me were written in your book before one of them came to be.

Almighty God, I thank You for creating me. Thank You, too, for the beauty of creation all around me. I have such limited understanding of You and Your creation. Out of nothing, You created everything. You SPOKE everything into existence.

Colossians 1:16 (NASB) says:
For by Him all things were created, BOTH in the heavens and on earth, visible and invisible, whether thrones or dominions or rulers or authorities -- all things have been created through Him and for Him.

Creator God, as I spend time thinking about You and Your creative power, I'm overwhelmed. Even now, in my mind I'm hearing one of my spiritual heroes, George Beverly Shea, sing these beautiful words from "How Great Thou Art," penned by Stuart K. Hine:

O Lord, My God, when I in awesome wonder,
Consider all the worlds Thy hands have made.
I see the stars; I hear the rolling thunder.
Thy power throughout the universe displayed.

Then sings my soul, my Savior, God to Thee,
How great Thou art, how great Thou art.
Then sings my soul, my Savior, God to Thee,
How great Thou art, how great Thou art.

And when I think that God, His Son not sparing
Sent Him to die, I scarce can take it in,
That on the cross, my burdens gladly bearing,
He bled and died to take away my sin.

Then sings my soul, my Savior, God to Thee,
How great Thou art, how great Thou art.
Then sings my soul, my Savior, God to Thee,
How great Thou art, how great Thou art.

When Christ shall come, with shout of acclamation
To take me home, what joy shall fill my heart,
And I shall bow in humble adoration
And there proclaim, my God, how great Thou art.

Then sings my soul, my Savior, God to Thee,
How great Thou art, how great Thou art.
Then sings my soul, my Savior, God to Thee,
How great Thou art, how great Thou art.

Blessings,
Don

God, I praise You for being

Elohim
____

God, I thank You for

My husband - My Children - My GrandKids
____

Father God, help me this year to

Draw nearer to You!
____

Daily Praise Moment

January 2

Praising Our "More Than Able" God

Jeremiah, whose words are recorded in Jeremiah 32:17 (NIV) says it well:
Ah, sovereign Lord, You have made the heavens and the earth by Your great power and outstretched arm. Nothing is too hard for You.

Jeremiah 32:27 (NIV) records God's response back to Jeremiah:
I am the LORD, the God of all mankind. Is anything too hard for me?

As we praise the LORD today, let's remember that NOTHING is too difficult for God.

I'm remembering Daniel's friends, Shadrach, Meshach and Abednego, as I reflect on the words of a song our church choir sometimes sings, "God Is Able," (words and music penned by Chris Machen and Robert Sterling, arranged by Carol Cymbala):

God is able. God is able - to deliver from the fire.
He will rescue those who serve Him,
When the flames are burning higher and higher and higher.
God Is Able.

Blessings,
Don

Almighty God, I praise You for:

A new year
____

____

Daily Praise Moment

January 3

Praising God by Walking in the Spirit

Romans 8:14 (NIV) says:
Those who are led by the Spirit of God are sons of God.

As we praise God today, we do well to remember that when we invited the Lord Jesus Christ to be our Savior and Lord, His Holy Spirit came to live in us. **We are indwelt by the very Spirit of God.**

Paul was inspired by the Holy Spirit of God who lived inside him to write to the Christians at Galatia and tell them of this major truth, recorded in Galatians 5:16 (NIV):
So I say, live by the Spirit, and you will not gratify the desires of the sinful nature.

As I reflect on today's Scripture, my musical mind begins hearing: "Holy Spirit, Thou Art Welcome," by Dottie Rambo and David Huntsinger, and "Spirit of the Living God," by Daniel Iverson.

Holy Spirit, Thou art welcome in this place.
Holy Spirit, Thou art welcome in this place.
Omnipotent Father of mercy and grace,
Thou art welcome in this place.

Spirit of the Living God, fall fresh on me.
Spirit of the Living God, fall fresh on me.
Melt me, mold me, fill me, use me.
Spirit of the Living God, fall fresh on me.

Blessings,
Don

Daily Praise Moment

January 4

Praising Jehovah God – The Self-Existing One

Revelation 1:8 (NKJV) says:
"I am the Alpha and the Omega, the Beginning and the End," says the Lord, "who is and who was and who is to come, the Almighty."

As interesting as it is for us to "find our roots" and learn about family history, we must remember that God has ALWAYS been and ALWAYS will be. There has never been a time when Jehovah God did not exist.

We have the unique privilege of having a vibrant relationship with Jehovah God, the Self-Existing One. Rather than trying to develop and implement my own plan for my life today, my goal is to yield the throne of my life to the Self-Existing One and let His plan be the one I follow today.

As I give thought to today's Scripture, my mind drifts back to a Christian music conference that my wife, Janet, and I attended several years ago. After breakfast, a young couple came forward and sang a simple little chorus that spoke deeply to my heart. The words, as best I remember them are:

You have always Been,
You will always Be,
And through eternity,
You Are.

Higher than the sky,
Deeper than the sea,
And Greater than the greatest,
By far.

Blessings,
Don

Author unknown

Daily Praise Moment

January 5

Praising God: My Strength, My Song and My Salvation

Exodus 15:2 (NIV) says:
Moses and the Israelites sang this song to the Lord: "The Lord is my strength and my song; and He has become my salvation."

I Chronicles 22:13 (NKJV) says:
Then you will prosper, if you take care to fulfill the statutes and judgments with which the LORD charged Moses concerning Israel. Be strong and of good courage; do not fear nor be dismayed.

Times come in our lives when we want to yield to fear; but God, our strength, lives inside us, and He wants us to live our lives trusting Him to meet all our needs.

Two beautiful choruses come to mind as I reflect on today's Scripture: "I Sing Praises," written by Terry MacAlmon (first chorus) and "Be Strong and Take Courage," by Don Moen.

I sing praises to Your name, O LORD, praises to Your name, O
LORD, for Your name is great and greatly to be praised. I give glory to
Your name, O LORD, glory to Your name, O LORD,
for Your name is great and greatly to be praised.

Be strong and take courage. Do not fear or be dismayed.
For the Lord will go before you, and His light will show the way.
Be strong and take courage. Do not fear or be dismayed.
For the one who lives within you will be strong in you today.

Blessings,
Don

Daily Praise Moment

January 6

Praising Our God Most High

Psalm 97:9 (NIV) says:
You, O Lord, are the Most High over all the earth; You are exalted far above all gods.

Across the years, I've been blessed to view mountain scenes that are truly captivating. Standing on the Foothills Parkway in Blount County, Tennessee, looking at the town of Maryville and McGhee Tyson Airport on one side and Miller's Cove on the other makes you feel so much closer than you feel when you're driving. Your whole perspective changes when you see things from above.

On a few occasions, we've been out West. From atop Mt. Moran or Pike's Peak, the view goes on for miles. An object that appears close may actually be 50 or more miles away!

As wonderful as it is for us to see far more than we've seen before, our Most High God sees it ALL. We are not just serving a Babe placed in a Manger; we're serving the Most High God. He is above and beyond every need we have.

My prayer at the moment is a prayer of praise.

Heavenly Father,
You are my Provider (Jehovah Jireh), my Healer (Jehovah Rophe) and my Banner (Jehovah Nissi). You, Lord God, are El Elyon – the Lord Most High – King of kings and Lord of lords, and I praise You. Amen

As I give thought to today's Scripture, my musical mind begins to hear, "Lord, We Praise You," by Otis Skillings:

Lord, we praise You. Lord, we praise You.
Lord, we praise You. We praise You, Lord.

Lord, we love You. Lord, we love You.
Lord, we love You. We love You, Lord.
Lord, we thank You. Lord, we thank You.

Lord, we thank You. We thank You, Lord.

Alleluia! Alleluia! Alleluia!
We give You praise.

Blessings,
Don

Daily Praise Moment

January 7

Praising Our "Always There" GOD

Psalm 139:7-12 (NASB) gives assurance that God is ALWAYS there with us:

7 *Where can I go from Your Spirit?*
Or where can I flee from Your presence?
8 *If I ascend to heaven, You are there;*
If I make my bed in Sheol, behold, You are there.
9 *If I take the wings of the dawn,*
If I dwell in the remotest part of the sea,
10 *Even there Your hand will lead me,*
And Your right hand will lay hold of me.
11 *If I say, "Surely the darkness will overwhelm me,*
And the light around me will be night,"
12 *Even the darkness is not dark to You,*
And the night is as bright as the day.
Darkness and light are alike to You.

As I think on these assuring words from Scripture, my musical mind races back to a song from my childhood, "Never Alone," words by Ludie Pickett (1897):

I've seen the lightning flashing, I've heard the thunder roll. I've felt sin's breakers dashing, which almost conquered my soul. I've heard the voice of my Savior, bidding me still to fight on. He promised never to leave me, never to leave me alone! No, never alone, no never alone, He promised never to leave me, He'll claim me for His own; no, never alone, no never alone. He promised never to leave me, never to leave me alone.

The world's fierce winds are blowing, temptation sharp and keen. I have a peace in knowing my Savior stands between— He stands to shield me from danger when my friends are all gone. He promised never to leave me, never to leave me alone!
No, never alone, no never alone, He promised never to leave me, He'll claim me for His own; no, never alone, no never alone. He promised never to leave me, never to leave me alone.

When in affliction's valley, I tread the road of care,
My Savior helps me carry the cross so heavy to bear;
Though all around me is darkness, earthly joys all flown;
My Savior whispers His promise, never to leave me alone!
No, never alone, no never alone, He promised never to leave me,
He'll claim me for His own; no, never alone, no never alone.
He promised never to leave me, never to leave me alone.

He died on Calvary's mountain, for me they piercèd His side.
For me He opened that fountain, the crimson, cleansing tide.
For me He waiteth in glory, seated upon His throne.
He promised never to leave me, never to leave me alone!
No, never alone, no never alone, He promised never to leave me,
He'll claim me for His own; no, never alone, no never alone.
He promised never to leave me, never to leave me alone.

Blessings,
Don

Public Domain.

Heavenly Father,
Thank You that we're never alone, for You, Almighty GOD, are always there with us.
AMEN

Daily Praise Moment

January 8

Praising GOD: Our Love, Our Light and Our Wisdom

Ephesians 5:1-2; 8-11; 15-21 (NKJV) has three themes:

Walk in Love
1 Therefore be imitators of God as dear children. 2 And walk in love, as
Christ also has loved us and given Himself for us, an offering and a
sacrifice to God for a sweet-smelling aroma.

Walk in Light
8 For you were once darkness, but now you are light in the Lord. Walk
as children of light 9 (for the fruit of the Spirit is in all goodness,
righteousness, and truth), 10 finding out what is acceptable to the Lord.
11 And have no fellowship with the unfruitful works of darkness, but
rather expose them.

Walk in Wisdom
15 See then that you walk circumspectly, not as fools but as wise, 16
redeeming the time, because the days are evil. 17 Therefore do not be
unwise, but understand what the will of the Lord is. 18 And do not be
drunk with wine, in which is dissipation; but be filled with the Spirit, 19
speaking to one another in psalms and hymns and spiritual songs,
singing and making melody in your heart to the Lord, 20 giving thanks
always for all things to God the Father in the name of our Lord Jesus
Christ, 21 submitting to one another in the fear of God.

God's Holy Word calls us to follow our Example, the Lord Jesus Christ, walking in His love, His light and His wisdom. Doing so can put us at odds with the mores that are commonly practiced in our society, but the bigger question for us is not, "What will my friends and family think if I take a position that is not the same as theirs?" The bigger question is, "What is God, through His Word and His indwelling Holy Spirit, calling me to do?"

My prayer today is this:

Heavenly Father,
Forgive me for just "going with the flow." I repent of taking control of my own life. You are Almighty God, and You know the path You

want me to follow. Thank You for Your forgiveness. Please work in me and through me to make me the servant You want me to be in Your kingdom. In the name that is above every name, the Lord Jesus Christ. AMEN

As I give thought to today's Scriptures, my musical mind begins to hear the chorus of the song, "Jesus, The Light of the World," written by George Elderkin:

Walk in the Light.
Jesus, the Light.
Come where the dewdrops
Of mercy shine bright.
Shine all around us,
By day and by night,
Jesus, the Light of the world.

I love you, and God loves you more!
Blessings,
Don

Public Domain

Father God, help me "walk in love" today as I:

____

Holy Father, thank You that I no longer have to walk in darkness. Help me keep my life clean so Your Light can clearly shine through me today as I seek to accomplish:

____

Righteous Father, in Jesus' name I ask You to help me listen to Your voice of wisdom as I walk through these challenges today:

____

Daily Praise Moments

January 9

Praising Our God Who Is Far Greater Than We Can Ever Know or Understand

Isaiah 40:28 (NLT), says:
Have you never heard? Have you never understood? The Lord is the everlasting God, the Creator of all the earth. He never grows weak or weary. No one can measure the depths of his understanding.

Paul, in writing to believers in Philippi, wrote these words recorded in Philippians 3:10 (NKJV):
"... that I may know Him and the power of His resurrection, and the fellowship of His sufferings, being conformed to His death. ..."

If we could hear the believers in Philippi talking to Paul, we might catch them saying, "What do you mean, you want to know Christ? You do know Christ! You even introduced us to Him."

But Paul might reply with these words: "Yes, I know Him a little bit, but don't you get it? I really want to KNOW Him. I know the only way I can really know Him and understand the power of His resurrection is to fellowship with Him in His sufferings, even if it means being conformed to His death."

I've been a believer for lots of years, but daily I am confronted with the reality that I'm standing only ankle deep in God's mighty ocean of Truth. I truly want to know Him, and I know you do, too, or you wouldn't be reading this!

As I reflect on today's Scriptures, my musical mind begins hearing "God and God Alone," a beautiful song written by Phill McHugh recorded by Steve Green contains these majestic lyrics:

God, and God alone, created all these things we call our own.
From the mighty to the small, the Glory in them all is God's,
And God's alone.

God, and God alone, reveals the truth of all we call unknown,
And all the best and worst of man won't change the Master's plan,
It's God's and God's alone.

God, and God alone, is fit to take the universe's throne.
Let everything that lives, reserve its truest praise
For God, and God alone.

God, and God alone, will be the joy of our eternal home.
He will be our one desire. Our hearts will never tire
Of God, and God alone.

God, and God alone, reveals the truth of all we call unknown,
And all the best and worst of man won't change the Master's plan,
It's God's and God's alone.

God, and God alone, is fit to take the universe's throne.
Let everything that lives, reserve its truest praise
For God, and God alone.

Blessings,
Don

Heavenly Father,
Please forgive me for ever allowing anything to take precedence over You. I yield my all to You today. Open my spiritual eyes, ears and heart to see, hear and understand Your divine majesty.

I pray this prayer in the strong and mighty name of Your Son and my Savior, the Lord Jesus Christ.
Amen

Daily Praise Moment

January 10

Praising Jehovah Shalom -- Our God Who Is Our Peace

Isaiah 9:6 (NKJV) says:
6 For unto us a Child is born,
Unto us a Son is given;
And the government will be upon His shoulder.
And His name will be called Wonderful, Counselor, Mighty God,
Everlasting Father, ***Prince of Peace****.* (emphasis added)

Jesus Christ, the Prince of Peace, as prophesied in Isaiah 9:6, is Jehovah Shalom. Shalom, a Hebrew word often translated as peace, means much, much more. In addition to peace, it conveys completeness, welfare, well-being and safety.

We experience the peace of God by following (heeding) the commands of God. As we "walk in the Spirit," our Prince of Peace lives out His peace in us.

Ephesians 6:13-15 (NKJV) says:
13 Therefore take up the whole armor of God, that you may be able to withstand in the evil day, and having done all, to stand.
14 Stand therefore, having girded your waist with truth, having put on the breastplate of righteousness, ***15 and having shod your feet with the preparation of the gospel of peace….*** (emphasis added)

God's peace flows through us, giving comfort to others and to us.

As I give thought to today's Scriptures, my musical mind begins to hear the old gospel hymn, "Wonderful Peace," written in 1889 by Warren D. Cornell (words) and W. George Cooper (music).

Far away in the depths of my spirit tonight
Rolls a melody sweeter than psalm;
In celestial strains it unceasingly falls
O'er my soul like an infinite calm.

Peace, peace, wonderful peace,
Coming down from the Father above!
Sweep over my spirit forever, I pray

In fathomless billows of love!

What a treasure I have in this wonderful peace,
Buried deep in the heart of my soul,
So secure that no power can mine it away,
While the years of eternity roll!

Peace, peace, wonderful peace,
Coming down from the Father above!
Sweep over my spirit forever, I pray
In fathomless billows of love!

Shalom,
Don

Public Domain

Heavenly Father,
Thank You for being Jehovah Shalom. Thank You for sending Your Son, the Lord Jesus Christ, to be our Savior. Thank You that when Christ arose, He broke sin's control over us.

Thank You that prior to Jesus' return to Heaven, He promised His followers that He would send the Holy Spirit to indwell us.

Thank You that we who are believers are indwelt by the Prince of Peace. We need no longer walk in fear for we are indwelt by Jehovah Shalom.

Forgive me, Father, for those times when I've forgotten the One to whom I belong. I'm sorry that I've sometimes yielded to fear. Thank You for Your forgiveness.

Help me, this day, to remember that You are my peace, my completeness, my well-being provider and my shield of safety.

I pray this prayer in the strong and mighty name of Jesus Christ.
AMEN

Daily Praise Moment

January 11

Praising God, Our Ever Present Protector and Provider (Part 1)

Psalm 91:9-11 (NKJV) says:
9 Because you have made the LORD, WHO IS my refuge, EVEN the
Most High, your dwelling place, 10 No evil shall befall you, Nor shall
any plague come near your dwelling; 11 For He shall give His angels
charge over you, To keep you in all your ways.

Several years ago, I was driving home from Nashville. It was our wedding anniversary and I had promised my wife, Janet, that we would go to one of her favorite restaurants to celebrate – Chesapeake's. I was driving my white Jeep Cherokee that had more than 200,000 miles on it, making good time and coming up the mountain from Cookeville, Tennessee, toward Monterey. Suddenly, steam was coming out from under the hood of my car. I was on time, but not very far ahead of schedule. My heart began to sink. Should I call Janet and tell her?

About the time I raised the hood, a light blue Chevy Camaro with the T-Tops out passed, slowed down, and backed down the hill toward me. A very muscular, skinny guy with no shoes or shirt got out of the car. His body was covered with dragon tattoos, front and back. He was missing a front tooth. I didn't know if I was about to be robbed or helped. This guy looked at my car, then asked if I had a knife. I wasn't sure about his motive, but reluctantly, I said, "yes." I gave him my state-issued, 20 years of service award pocket knife.

He took my knife, cut the top water hose off my radiator, shortened it, and reattached it. He then proceeded to his Camaro, popped open the trunk and pulled out two containers – a gallon of water and a gallon of antifreeze. Within 10 minutes, he had my car running again. Then, he followed me up the mountain to the auto parts store where I was able to buy a new radiator hose and antifreeze. When I tried to pay him for his help, he refused. He said that someone had once helped him, and he carried the water and antifreeze to return the favor. I told him that I didn't know angels had dragon tattoos, but he had been an angel to me. He said he had been in Special Forces in the military and got the tattoos while doing karate training.

I praise God for meeting my need in such a unique way. My musical mind, reflecting on this event, hears a song from my childhood that I'm sure you remember:

All night all day, angels watchin' over me, my Lord,
All night all day, angels watchin' over me.

Day is dyin' the west, angels watchin' over me, my Lord
Sleep my child and take your rest, angels watchin' over me.

All night all day, angels watchin' over me, my Lord.
All night all day, angels watchin' over me.

Now I lay me down to sleep, angels watchin' over me, my Lord.
I pray the Lord my soul to keep, angels watchin' over me.

All night all day, angels watchin' over me, my Lord.
All night all day, angels watchin' over me.

Blessings,
Don

Public Domain

Heavenly Father,
In Jesus' name I thank You for previously taking care of me when:

____

____

In faith, I thank You for Your watchful care today as I:

____

____

I pray this prayer in the strong and mighty name of Jesus Christ.
Amen

Daily Praise Moment

January 12

Praising God, Our Ever Present Protector and Provider (Jehovah Shammah) Part 2

Psalm 91:9-11 NKJV says:
9 Because you have made the LORD, WHO IS my refuge, EVEN the Most High, your dwelling place, 10 No evil shall befall you, Nor shall any plague come near your dwelling; 11 For He shall give His angels charge over you, To keep you in all your ways....

Much happens around us that we rarely recognize. I believe our Heavenly Father is on guard for us at all times, and we are going to be very surprised when we get to heaven and learn of all He has done that we never noticed. I'm thrilled to know that our Savior, Jehovah Shammah, is ALWAYS present with us.

As I reflect on the same verses today as yesterday, my mind drifts back to another incident where God was clearly with us. In the late 1970s, Janet and I had a young couple over for dinner at our home. They were the proud owners of a brand new Volkswagen Rabbit, similar to the one we had been driving for two or three years. We enjoyed our dinner and fellowship. We swapped stories and talked on until about 10 p.m. When this couple got ready to leave, for some reason unknown to me at that time, I went downstairs, raised the garage door, turned on the water, and began washing my little car. I'm telling them "goodbye" as I am squirting water on my red Volkswagen Rabbit. When they fired up their new little VW Rabbit, smoke began to rise from under the hood. We quickly raised the hood and saw blue flames coming from the engine. I immediately turned the water hose on the fire and it went out. Praise the Lord!!!

Their car was parked next to my VW Rabbit, which had about 10 gallons of gas in it. On the other side of their new little Rabbit was Janet's Chevy, which had a 20-plus-gallon tank that was full. All three cars were adjacent to our home!

I believe that Jehovah Shammah, our ever-present Lord, does these kinds of miracles for us all the time, but I know that I often fail to recognize His hand of protection around me.

As I think on today's Scripture is “He Is Here, He Is Here,” written by Jimmy Owens, which has these enchanting words:

He is here, He is here. He is moving among us.
He is here, He is here, as we gather in His name.
He is here, He is here, and He wants to work a wonder.
He is here, as we gather in His name.

He is Lord, He is Lord, let us worship before Him.
He is Lord, He is Lord, as we gather in His name.
He is Lord, He is Lord, let us praise and adore Him –
Yesterday and today and forevermore the same.

Blessings,
Don

Father God,
Thank You for being Jehovah Shammah, our ever-present Provider. You never leave us and we are always in Your care.

Thank You, thank You, thank You.

We pray this prayer in the strong and mighty name of Your Son and our Savior, Jesus Christ.
Amen

Daily Praise Moment

January 13

Praising The Lord Who Cleanses Us Whiter Than Snow (Part 1)

Psalm 51:7 (NKJV) says:
[7] *Purge me with hyssop, and I shall be clean;*
Wash me, and I shall be whiter than snow.

When I was a child, we heated our home with a "Warm Morning" coal stove. The coal and scrap wood kindling piles were not the prettiest spots around our home, except when it snowed. All the blackness of the coal disappeared under the beautiful white covering.

Fresh snow gives us a glimpse of God's cleansing forgiveness. However, snow only lasts for a short while. Then, it melts away.

Not so with God's cleansing. It is complete and eternal!

As we think about the beauty of fresh-fallen snow, let's reflect on the beauty of the cleansing that Our Lord Jesus Christ bought for us when He shed His blood to pay our sin penalty.

I know that you love the words of this familiar song, "Whiter Than Snow," penned by James L. Nicholson and published in 1872:

Lord Jesus, I long to be perfectly whole;
I want Thee forever to live in my soul;
Break down every idol, cast out every foe.
Now wash me, and I shall be whiter than snow.

Whiter than snow, yes, whiter than snow,
Now wash me, and I shall be whiter than snow.

Lord Jesus, let nothing unholy remain,
Apply Thine own blood and extract every stain;
To get this blest cleansing, I all things forego.
Now wash me, and I shall be whiter than snow.

Whiter than snow, yes, whiter than snow,
Now wash me, and I shall be whiter than snow.

Lord Jesus, look down from Thy throne in the skies,
And help me to måke a complete sacrifice;
I give up myself, and whatever I know ——
Now wash me, and I shall be whiter than snow.

Whiter than snow, yes, whiter than snow,
Now wash me, and I shall be whiter than snow.

Lord Jesus, for this I most humbly entreat,
I wait, blessed Lord, at Thy crucified feet.
By faith for my cleansing, I see thy blood flow ——
Now wash me, and I shall be whiter than snow.

Blessings,
Don

Personal Thoughts:

____

____

____

____

Daily Praise Moment

January 14

Praising The Lord Who Cleanses Us Whiter than Snow (Part 2)

Psalm 51:7 (NKJV) says:
Purge me with hyssop, and I shall be clean;
Wash me, and I shall be whiter than snow.

The word, hyssop, which appears in this verse, occurs 12 times in the Bible. The first is in Exodus 12:22, where Moses is told to use hyssop to paint the blood of the Passover lamb over the lintel and doorposts of every Jewish home so the Death Angel would pass over.

In John's gospel, in the Scriptures dealing with Jesus' crucifixion, the word, hyssop, appears again. In John 19:28, Jesus says, *"I thirst."* In verse 29, John says that a branch of hyssop was used to lift a sponge full of sour wine to Jesus' lips. Mark's gospel reports that the sour wine was mixed with myrrh. Remember that myrrh was one of the gifts given to Jesus by the Wise Men. Mark also records that Jesus refused to take the pain-killing drink. Jesus bore our pain and carried our sorrows.

Isaiah 53:4-6 (NASB) says:
4 *Surely our griefs He Himself bore,*
And our sorrows He carried;
Yet we ourselves esteemed Him stricken,
Smitten of God, and afflicted.
5 *But He was pierced through for our transgressions,*
He was crushed for our iniquities;
The chastening for our well-being fell upon Him,
And by His scourging we are healed.
6 *All of us like sheep have gone astray,*
Each of us has turned to his own way;
But the LORD has caused the iniquity of us all
To fall on Him.

The blood of Jesus, our Passover Lamb, was spread over all believers, protecting us from the Death Angel. John 19:30 records Jesus' words, *"It is finished."*

Indeed, He finished paying a debt we could never repay.

As I think on today's Scriptures, my musical mind jumps to a chorus by Ellis J. Crum which has these words:

He paid the debt He did not owe;
I owed a debt I could not pay.
I needed someone to wash my sins away.
But now, I sing a brand new song, Amazing Grace.
Christ Jesus paid a debt that I could never pay.

Blessings,
Don

Heavenly Father,
Thank You for forgiving me. I'm sorry for those times when I yield to unbelief and carry the load of guilt from sins I've already confessed to You. Doing so means that I'm listening to Satan's accusations of me and denying the sufficiency of Your promise to forgive my sins when I honestly confess them to You.

Thank You for giving me the strength to rebuke the enemy, Satan, when he tries to accuse me. Thank You for giving me the strength to walk away from the temptations Satan places in my path.

I love You.

Amen

Daily Praise Moment

January 15

Praising The Lord Who Is Our Strength and Our Shield

Psalm 28:7 (NIV) says:
The Lord is my strength and my shield;
My heart trusts in Him and He helps me.
My heart leaps for joy, and with my song I praise Him.

What a wonderful verse for today. The Lord IS my strength and my shield. He is totally trustworthy. My personal prayer is that my heart would fully, completely and submissively trust Him with every detail of my life.

Looking back over my life, I see that our Lord Jesus Christ HAS helped me all the way. Even when the way was very dark, He was still there for me, giving me the strength I needed. And, He is still there, shielding me from the dangers around me.

As I mull over these truths and think about how God has been there with me and worked things out on my behalf, joy rises in my heart. My hope and prayer is that I will remember God's goodness and always have a song of praise on my lips, honoring Him for who He is and thanking Him for how He has strengthened and shielded me from Satan's attempts to harm me.

In thinking about today's Scripture, my musical mind begins hearing "Praise the Lord" by Brown Bannister and Mike Hudson, which has these powerful lyrics:

When you're up against a struggle
That shatters all your dreams,
And your hopes have been cruelly crushed
By Satan's manifested schemes.
And you feel the urge within you
To submit to earthly fears,
Don't let the faith you're standin' in
Seem to disappear.
Praise the Lord,
He can work through those who praise Him.

Praise the Lord,
For our God inhabits praise.
Praise the Lord,
For the chains that seem to bind you
Serve only to remind you
That they drop powerless behind you
When you praise Him.

Now, Satan is a liar,
And he wants to make us think
That we are paupers when he knows himself
We're children of the King.
So lift up the mighty shield of faith
For the battle must be won.
We know that Jesus Christ is risen,
So the work's already done.

Praise the Lord,
He can work through those who praise Him.
Praise the Lord,
For our God inhabits praise.
Praise the Lord,
For the chains that seem to bind you
Serve only to remind you
That they drop powerless behind you
When you praise Him.

Blessings,
Don

Daily Praise Moment

January 16

Praising The Lord Who Is Our Protector

Ephesians 6:11 (NKJV) says:
Put on the whole armor of God that you may be able to stand against the wiles of the devil.

We are in the midst of a battle, and the enemy is Satan himself.

John 10:10 (NKJV) tell us:
The thief does not come except to steal, and to kill, and to destroy. I have come that they may have life, and that they may have it more abundantly.

Sometimes, we get caught up in the moment and lose sight of the real enemy. It is important for us to remember that all people are highly valued by God. As we clothe ourselves in the full armor of God (Ephesians 6:11-15), we are equipped to stand firm against the tricks and deceptions of the devil. We walk in the protection that God gives us.

Romans 13:12 (NKJV) says:
The night is far spent, the day is at hand. Therefore let us cast off the works of darkness, and let us put on the armor of light.

Today and every day, God is reminding me that I have a choice – to walk in darkness or to be clothed with His armor of light. Jesus is the Light of the World, and He lives inside all of us who are believers. My prayer is that I will allow God to keep my globe clean so others can see the Light of the World.

We all remember the children's song, "This Little Light of Mine."

This little light of mine, I'm gonna let it shine!
This little light of mine, I'm gonna let it shine!
This little light of mine, I'm gonna let it shine!

Let it shine, let it shine, let it shine!
Hide it under a bushel, NO! I'm gonna let it shine!
Hide it under a bushel, NO! I'm gonna let it shine!

Hide it under a bushel, NO! I'm gonna let it shine!

Let it shine, let it shine, let it shine!

Let it shine till Jesus comes, I'm gonna let it shine!
Let it shine till Jesus comes, I'm gonna let it shine!
Let it shine till Jesus comes, I'm gonna let it shine!

Let it shine, let it shine, let it shine!

Blessings,
Don

Public Domain

Lord Jesus,
As we let Your light shine in this dark world, You make a difference, both in our lives and in the lives of those who associate with us.

Thank You for giving us the privilege of being tools that You can use to bring light to the world.
AMEN

Daily Praise Moment

January 17

Praising Our God Who Never Leaves Us

Romans 8:38-39 (NIV) says:
[38]*For I am convinced that neither death nor life, neither angels nor demons, neither the present nor the future, nor any powers,* [39]*neither height nor depth, nor anything else in all creation, will be able to separate us from the love of God that is in Christ Jesus our Lord.*

When I was a child (10 or 11 years old), I sensed God calling me to confess my sins and yield control of my life to Him – to be saved. I came forward during Vacation Bible School and was "saved." That night, I "camped out" on the roof of our "cabin," a shed attached to the back of our family garage, located across the creek from our home. As I lay there on the roof looking at the stars, doubts filled my mind. I had expected the "salvation experience" of inviting Christ into my heart to be my Savior and Lord to result in me feeling like "shouting for joy." That feeling wasn't there, and I asked God, "Is this all there is? Do I really have a personal relationship with You? Am I really saved?"

When I was about 15, I came forward at church one Sunday and said, "I'm not sure I'm saved." My older brother, Bill, came to me and said, "Donnie, what are you doing here? You're saved already!" I thought that since he was older and wiser, he must be right, so I "rededicated" my life; however, the doubts continued to plague me.

One night after Janet and I were married, we were spending the night at her parents' home. I was watching Dr. Bill Bright, founder of Campus Crusade for Christ, on TV. He talked about God's love and how God wants to have a close, personal relationship with each of us. Dr. Bright presented his gospel message by going through a tract that he had written called "The 4 Spiritual Laws:"

Law 1 – God loves you and has a wonderful plan for your life.
Law 2 – Man is sinful and separated from God.
Law 3 – Christ's sin payment bridged the gap between us and God.
Law 4 – God invites us to accept Christ by personal invitation.

Then, Dr. Bright presented a prayer and was about to invite people to pray the prayer with him; however, he paused and said, "Some of you have prayed this prayer many times, but you lack assurance of salvation. I invite you to join me in praying the prayer one last time, then from this time forward, to thank God for being trustworthy and faithful to His promise to save you."

I joined Dr. Bright that night, invited Christ to come into my heart and be my Lord and Savior. Then, I thanked God for being faithful to His promise to save me if I would call upon Him with a sincere heart and invite Him to be my Lord. My doubts disappeared. Each time Satan would try to trick me, I'd tell him that I had a new owner, Jesus Christ. In reality, I'm not sure when my actual salvation occurred. While this change of ownership probably happened when I was a child, assurance only came after I began thanking and praising God for saving me. I hope you have assurance of your salvation. If you don't, please invite Christ in one last time, then thank Him for honoring the His Word. (Revelation 3:20).

As I mull on today's Scripture, my musical mind begins hearing the wonderful lyrics of "Now I Belong to Jesus," by Norman J. Clayton:

Jesus, my Lord, will love me forever, from Him no power of evil can sever. He gave His life to ransom my soul; now I belong to Him. Now I belong to Jesus. Jesus belongs to me. Not for the years of time alone, but for eternity.

Once I was lost in sin's degradation; Jesus came down to bring me salvation, lifted me up from sorrow and shame; now I belong to Him. Now I belong to Jesus. Jesus belongs to me. Not for the years of time alone, but for eternity.

Joy floods my soul, for Jesus has saved me, freed me from sin that long had enslaved me; His precious blood He gave to redeem. Now I belong to Him. Now I belong to Jesus. Jesus belongs to me. Not for the years of time alone, but for eternity.

Blessings,
Don

Daily Praise Moment

January 18

Praising Our God Who Meets Our Needs

Mark 11:24 (NASB), records our Lord's words to his disciples: *Therefore I say to you, all things for which you pray and ask, believe that you have received them, and they will be granted you.*

Matthew 7:7-11 (NASB) has these words, spoken by our Savior in the Sermon on the Mount:
7 Ask, and it will be given to you; seek, and you will find; knock, and it
will be opened to you. 8 For everyone who asks receives, and he who
seeks finds, and to him who knocks, it will be opened. 9 Or what man is
there among you who, when his son asks for a loaf, will give him a
stone? 10 Or if he asks for a fish, he will not give him a snake, will he?
11 If you then, being evil, know how to give good gifts to your children,
how much more will your Father who is in heaven give what is good to
those who ask Him!

Aren't you glad that we serve a God who is faithful, answers our prayers and meets our needs? He isn't a despot who just wants our service. His heart is focused on us, and He cares about every detail of our lives! Likewise, He wants us to focus on Him! I'm sure that the blessings He offers us are far more than we ever experience because we often fail to seek His heart. It saddens me to think about a future time in Heaven when I'll learn about all He had planned for me that I never experienced because I didn't seek His heart or follow His direction.

Several years ago I heard a story of a young man who gave his elderly uncle a chain saw for Christmas. About a month later, the young man visited his uncle and asked about how he liked the chain saw. The uncle said, "It's pretty, but it doesn't work very well for me – cutting trees is easier with my old saw." The young man said, "Let me look at it and see what's wrong." He checked the saw, pulled the starter cable and when it fired up, his uncle jumped backwards and screamed, "What in the world is that loud noise?"

As I think about today's Scriptures, my musical mind begins to hear "Seek Ye First," written by Karen Lafferty, which has these lyrics:

Seek ye first the Kingdom of God and His righteousness,
And all these things shall be added unto you, allelu, alleluia.

Ask and it shall be given unto you, seek and ye shall find,
Knock and the door shall be opened unto you, allelu, alleluia.

Blessings,
Don

Father God,
Forgive me for the many times when I don't seek You with all my heart.

As I go about my activities today, remind me of the chain saw story so I will see that You have so much more for me if I will simply listen and honestly apply Your principles to my life.

I love You and I want to love you more.

I pray this prayer in the name which is above every name, the Lord Jesus Christ.
Amen

Personal Thoughts:

____

____

____

Daily Praise Moment

January 19

Praising The Lord Who Fashioned Us In Our Mother's Womb

Psalm 139:13-16 (NASB) says:
13 For You formed my inward parts; You wove me in my mother's womb. 14 I will give thanks to You, for I am fearfully and wonderfully made; Wonderful are Your works, And my soul knows it very well. 15 My frame was not hidden from You, When I was made in secret, AND skillfully wrought in the depths of the earth; 16 Your eyes have seen my unformed substance; And in Your book were all written The days that were ordained FOR ME, When as yet there was not one of them.

In 1984, President Reagan issued a proclamation designating Sunday, January 22, 1984, the 11th anniversary of Roe v. Wade, as National Sanctity of Human Life Day. Since then, the Sunday closest to January 22 has been deemed by many Christians as an appropriate time to commemorate "Sanctity of Life Sunday." The verses from Psalm 139 poetically describe God's grand creation of you and me! Like a beautiful tapestry, we are woven by God. And, as verse 14 says, we are fearfully and wonderfully made. Verse 16 reminds us that before we breathed our first breath, God wrote our days in His book. He made us, and He is STILL perfecting His creation.

Romans 12:1-2 (NASB) says:
1 Therefore I urge you, brethren, by the mercies of God, to present your bodies a living and holy sacrifice, acceptable to God, WHICH IS your spiritual service of worship. 2 And do not be conformed to this world, ***but be transformed by the renewing of your mind, so that you may prove what the will of God is, that which is good and acceptable and perfect.*** (emphasis added)

God is STILL forming us into the likeness of Christ. Remember the saying? "I'm not what I used to be. I'm not what I want to be. But, Thank God, I'm not what I was."

About ten years ago, God gave me a specific task to do: Tell each mother of a baby or small child how beautiful their baby is, and then say, "Children are a gift of the Lord."

The Lord Jesus Christ loves ALL children. And, He wants us to love them all, too. Remember the scene found in Matthew 19, where Jesus is teaching a large group of people. Jesus' disciples are trying to hear and to insure that everyone else hears. In their minds, the answer to the noise problem that the children are creating is to shush the children and send them away, but the children are being drawn to Jesus. In Matthew 19:14, Jesus reprimands His disciples, saying, *"Suffer the little children to come unto me and forbid them not, for such is the Kingdom of Heaven."*

Just as God values and fashions children, He is fashioning us, too.

As I think on today's Scriptures, my musical mind jumps to the children's song, "He's Still Working on Me" by Joel Hemphill:

He's still working on me,
To make me what I ought to be.
It took Him just a week to make the moon and stars,
The Sun and the Earth and Jupiter and Mars.
How loving and patient He must be,
He's still working on me.

There really ought to be a sign upon each heart,
Don't judge me yet, there's an unfinished part.
But I'll be perfect just according to His plan
Fashioned by the Master's loving hands.

He's still working on me,
To make me what I ought to be.
It took Him just a week to make the moon and stars,
The Sun and the Earth and Jupiter and Mars.
How loving and patient He must be,
He's still working on me.

Blessings,
Don

Daily Praise Moment

January 20

Praising Our All Knowing, All Caring Heavenly Father

Psalm 116:12 (NASB) says:
What shall I render to the LORD
For all His benefits toward me?

Psalm 116:17 has these words:
To You I shall offer a sacrifice of thanksgiving,
And call upon the name of the LORD.

I sometimes fail to see God's protection and care until years have passed. When the "light" finally comes on, I'm humbled and filled with thanksgiving.

In the spring of 1965, I was a senior at Loudon High School in Loudon, Tennessee. My physics class was very small, just five or six students. Our class was taught by the chemistry teacher, Mrs. Smith, and we met in the chemistry lab (that's another story for another day!!!). None of us were physics stars, and all of us looked for ways to talk our teacher into an alternative to a physics lesson.

One day, we "sold" Mrs. Smith on the idea of taking the entire class to the Health Department to be screened for tuberculosis. All of us piled into Mrs. Smith's car. We had a wonderful time – that is, until the test results came back. To my shock and horror, my test results were positive. When follow-up tests and multiple x-rays were done, I was diagnosed with TB. I graduated from high school on a Friday night, and on Monday morning, moved into a semi-private room at East Tennessee Chest Disease Hospital.

At the time, I felt like my world had flipped upside down and that I'd been abandoned. Looking back, though, I now see that this was God's way of protecting me. During my 50 days in the hospital, I came to learn a major truth about life that has stuck with me vividly – "All of us are terminally ill." One of the men in my hospital ward had been there for seven years. During my 50 days there, five of the men in my ward died. As a young man, I was forced to see life differently.

Thank God, my TB was caught early. I was put on limited activity for a year and taught to avoid things that would negatively impact my health. God used this "bad" situation to bring about good in my life.

As I think of today's verses, my musical mind begins to hear the beautiful hymn, "God Will Take Care of You," words by Civilla D. Martin and music by W. Stillman Martin:

Be not dismayed what-e'er be-tide.
God will take care of you.
Beneath His wings of love, abide.
God will take care of you.

God will take care of you,
Through every day, o'er all the way.
He will take care of you,
God will take care of you.

He certainly does, and I praise Him.

Blessings,
Don

Public Domain

Father God,
Thank You for protecting me today as I trust You to safely guide me through:

____

____

____

Daily Praise Moment

January 21

Praising Our God Who Has a Divine Plan for Each of Our Lives

Matthew 6:10 (NASB) says:
Thy will be done on earth as it is in Heaven.

The model prayer that Christ gave His disciples when they asked Him to teach them to pray is filled with nuggets of Truth that we're all still learning. For such a long time, I assumed that Matthew 6:10 was asking me to pray for people living outside of God's will. What God has been teaching me, though, is that this verse is aimed at ME. God wants me to do His will in my life, to follow His leading with the same obedience and fervency as those in Heaven are doing. The more I ponder this verse, the more I realize just how far I am from being submissive to God's will for my life.

Theologian Reinhold Niebuhr penned the Serenity Prayer, a prayer that has been adopted by Alcoholics Anonymous and other fine programs. A shortened form of this poem contains these words:

"God, grant me the Serenity to accept the things I cannot change, Courage to change the things I can, And Wisdom to know the difference."

I'm certainly impacted by these beautiful words; however, a take on Niebuhr's prayer that impacts me even more is this one, written by John G. Miller, author of "QBQ! *THE QUESTION BEHIND THE QUESTION*":

"God grant me the SERENITY to accept the people I cannot change, the COURAGE to change the one I can, and the WISDOM to know … It's me!"

As I mull over the intent of Matthew 6:10, my musical mind jumps to a Doug Holck song, "Your Love Compels Me," which has these powerful lyrics:

Your love compels me, Lord, to give as You would give,
To speak as You would speak, to live as You would live.

Your love compels me, Lord, to see as You would see,
To serve as You would serve, to be what You would be.

Blessings,
Don

Daily Praise Moment

January 22

Praising Our God Who Blesses Us in Unusual Ways

Psalm 145:3 (NASB) says:
Great is the Lord, and highly to be praised, His greatness is unsearchable.

My wife, Janet, and I have been blessed immeasurably across the years. On a few occasions, those blessings have come in the most unique, unusual ways.

Several years ago, during a Sunday night worship service, a lady entered our church sanctuary as the congregation was singing. Instead of sitting downstairs with everyone else, she went to the balcony where she could be alone. I had known this precious woman for a number of years, and I knew she had health issues – allergies that made it hard for her to associate with other people. It was rare to see her in church on Sundays, especially on Sunday evenings.

As we were singing, God burdened my heart for her. In His still small voice, which I admit that I had rarely listened to, the Holy Spirit of God clearly spoke to me and said, "Give her the money you have in your wallet."

As the pastor preached his sermon, I thought about this urge God had given me, but I tried to dismiss it. After the pastor finished preaching, I began leading the congregation in singing the invitation hymn and God repeated His command to me. This time I said "yes" to Him. I didn't know how much money was in my wallet, but as church ended and I walked out of the building, I took the money out of my billfold without looking at the amount, rolled it up and walked across the church parking lot to catch up with the lady before she could drive away. I gave her a hug and put the money in her hand.

When Janet and I arrived home about twenty minutes later, our phone was ringing. The woman from church was on the phone, crying profusely. After she calmed, she told me that her electricity was being turned off the next morning. She had contacted family and friends and scrapped together all she could, but she was still $21 short, or at least she had been until I handed her the money after church.

I'm sure you've figured it out by now. The mysterious amount of money I had in my wallet that night was $21 – the exact amount she needed.

That was years ago, but God is still using that event to bless my life. Also, He is using the memory of that night to challenge my heart and humble me. After all, He is God Supreme. All that I have is not really mine – it is HIS. He is Master, LORD, ALMIGHTY GOD, and my role is to be His obedient servant.

As I think on the today's Scripture, my musical mind begins to hear "Awesome God," by Rich Mullins, which has these wonderful lyrics:

Our God is an awesome God.
He reigns from Heaven above
With Wisdom, Power and Love.
Our God is an awesome God.

Blessings,
Don

Father God,
Help me keep my "spiritual ears" turned on so I can hear You speak to me. Remind me that as I attend to Your leadings, my life can have meaning and purpose and I can be a blessing to others. Thank You that you have called me to be Your ambassador, and everything I have is Yours. Therefore, I should never see giving as undesirable. In fact, I should see it as a privilege. I know that holding onto resources that You are telling me to give is disobedience. The best water comes from clear, mountain springs, not stagnant ponds. I know that as I trust You and give, You bless me even more!

I love you and pray this prayer in Jesus' name.
AMEN

Daily Praise Moment

January 23

Praising the Lord Our Banner (Jehovah – Nissi)

1 Chronicles 29:11-13 (NASB) says:
11Yours, O LORD, is the greatness and the power and the glory and the victory and the majesty, indeed everything that is in the heavens and the earth; Yours is the dominion, O LORD, and You exalt Yourself as head over all. 12 Both riches and honor COME from You, and You rule over all, and in Your hand is power and might; and it lies in Your hand to make great and to strengthen everyone. 13 Now therefore, our God, we thank You, and praise Your glorious name.

One of the Knoxville radio stations used to have a slogan that was repeated multiple times each day. The slogan was “Who’s Got You Now? WRJZ.” I listened to the station often as I drove home from work. Many times, God used that little teaser slogan to bring to mind my need to be following Him – to be under His Banner, to be 100 percent on His team.

As today's scripture clearly states, ALL greatness rightfully belongs to God. After all, HE is GOD. He has the greatness, power, glory, victory and majesty. He is head over all. His hand IS power and might. What a privilege we have of being part of His family! That privilege was extended to us when we invited Christ into our hearts to be our Savior and Lord (boss of our lives).

Psalm 60:4 (NASB) says:
You have given a banner to those who fear You, that it may be displayed because of the truth.

One of my dear friends is a "dyed in the wool" Alabama fan. The "A" on the front of his car used to be Alabama red, but the sun has taken its toll – the A is now bluish-purplish-brown. Giving him back a small dose of the medicine he has been giving me as a "Big Orange" fan, I asked him if the color changed when his team lost to another team inside his home state, or did it happen when the new assistant coach was hired.

You and I can start our journey as "true blue" followers of the Lord Jesus Christ, but we can yield to the daily stresses that come our way, and if we're not careful, our allegiance to our Savior can wane. Daily, our task is to yield to Christ's Lordship as we ask ourselves, "Who's Got You Now?"

As I think on today's Scriptures, my musical mind begins to hear the hymn "The Banner of the Cross," penned by Daniel Whittle in 1887:

There's a royal banner given for display
To the soldiers of the King.
As an ensign fair we lift it up today,
While as ransomed ones we sing.
Marching on, marching on,
For Christ count everything but loss!
And to crown Him King, we'll toil and sing
Beneath the banner of the cross!

Blessings,
Don

Public Domain

PS Have a wonderful day, brothers and sisters, as you follow our soon-coming Savior, walking under His royal banner.

Living my life under God's Banner can change the following aspects of my life:

____

____

____

____

Daily Praise Moment

January 24

Praising Our Ever-Present God – I AM

Exodus 3:13-14 (NASB) says:
Then Moses said to God, "Behold, I am going to the sons of Israel, and I will say to them, 'The God of your fathers has sent me to you.' Now they may say to me, 'What is His name?' What shall I say to them?" 14 *God said to Moses, "I AM WHO I AM"; and He said, "Thus you shall say to the sons of Israel, 'I AM has sent me to you.'"*

Moses was pasturing the sheep of his father-in-law, Jethro, when he came upon the burning bush. When he went to see why it wasn't burned up, the Holy Spirit of God spoke to him from the bush, telling him to remove his shoes for he was on "holy ground." God reminded Moses that His people were in bondage in Egypt. Then God told Moses to go and lead His people to safety.

Moses faced an overwhelming challenge. Pharaoh wanted to kill him, and he knew the Israelites would not trust him or be eager to follow him. The sky was dark on his horizon.

Many times we face problems that seem overwhelmingly scary – so large that we can't see anything but darkness – like being caught up in a major thunderstorm. Satan wants us to believe that God either doesn't know or doesn't care about us. But, as today's verses say, God certainly DOES KNOW and HE certainly DOES CARE.

Many years ago, I was leaving Knoxville on Tennessee Airways, flying to Nashville in an 18-passenger prop-jet. As we were boarding the plane that morning, the airport was in the middle of a major rainstorm. The grass in the field beside the runway was bent to the ground from the strong winds, and rain was pouring down in sheets. I prayed for safety, for the pilot and crew, and for the other passengers, but all I could see was the storm. As the plane took off, the winds made it feel like we were on a very bad ride in an amusement park.
A few minutes into the tumultuous flight, we broke through the clouds. Much to my surprise, the sun was brilliantly shining. Everything was beautiful. As I looked out the window in amazement, the Holy Spirit of God gave me a gentle nudge and said, "I've been here all the time. I'll never leave you."

God never has an "I DIDN'T KNOW THAT" moment. He isn't just the God who was "in the beginning" or the God who "will come again." He is our ever-present God, our Protector, our Companion and our Friend – the Great I AM.

As I reflect on today's Scriptures, my musical mind jumps to a song our choir sings, "The Great I AM Still Is," by Phil Cross and Twila LaBar, which has these beautiful lyrics:

Jerusalem's Deliverer, Divider of the sea,
The Conqueror of Jericho, Jehovah set them free.
Some think of Him as fable, with no relevance today,
But God's past power never passed away.

The Great I AM still is.
The heavens and the earth are His.
He's the Merciful Almighty, forever Holy.
In everything we must remember this:
The Great I AM still IS.

Blessings,
Don

Daily Praise Moment

January 25

Praising God for His Amazing Grace

Hebrews 4:14-16 (NASB) says:
[14] Therefore, since we have a great high priest who has passed through the heavens, Jesus the Son of God, let us hold fast our confession. [15]
For we do not have a high priest who cannot sympathize with our weaknesses, but One who has been tempted in all things as WE ARE, YET without sin. [16] Therefore, let us draw near with confidence to the throne of grace, so that we may receive mercy and find grace to help in time of need.

We've probably all heard the definition of grace that uses an acrostic: God's Riches At Christ's Expense. While this definition is very helpful, I'm not sure that it comes anywhere near plumbing the depths of what GRACE really means.

We always know we need God's grace during the hard times, like death, illness, and other life changing tragedies. However, God's grace extends to us at ALL times.

Grace is God's provision for my need, for your need.

Though God's grace is free, it is not cheap! It is important to not cheapen Grace by saying, "I can do as I wish, because I'm under God's grace."

Likewise, God doesn't want us to feel that Grace is limited to His saving us – that we must struggle on alone until Jesus returns for us. No, God's grace meets our needs every day.

We must have God's grace to survive. Philippians 2:13 says,
[13] for it is God who is at work in you, both to will and to work for HIS good pleasure.

We are desperately wicked (Jeremiah 4:14). Without Christ's atoning death for us and His constant intercession for us (Heb. 4:14-16), none of us would make it to Heaven. But, Thank God, we're going to Heaven if we are a follower of Jesus Christ – if we've trusted Christ to save us and are following Him. After all, because of His Amazing Grace, He is our Great High Priest who ever lives to make intercession for us.

As I meditate on today's Scriptures, my musical mind begins to hear "Grace Greater Than Our Sin," lyrics penned by Julia Johnson and music written by Daniel Towner in 1910:

Marvelous grace of our loving Lord, Grace that exceeds our sin and our guilt, yonder on Calvary's mount out-poured, there where the blood of the Lamb was spilt. Grace, grace, God's grace, Grace that will pardon and cleanse within; Grace, grace, God's grace, Grace that is greater than all our sin.

Sin and despair, like the sea waves cold, threaten the soul with infinite loss; Grace that is greater, yes, grace untold points to the refuge, the mighty cross. Grace, grace, God's grace, Grace that will pardon and cleanse within; Grace, grace, God's grace, Grace that is greater than all our sin.

Dark is the stain that we cannot hide, what can avail to wash it away? Look! There is flowing a crimson tied, whiter than snow you may be today. Grace, grace, God's grace, Grace that will pardon and cleanse within; Grace, grace, God's grace, Grace that is greater than all our sin.

Marvelous, infinite, matchless grace, freely bestowed on all who believe! You that are longing to see His face, will you this moment His grace receive. Grace, grace, God's grace, Grace that will pardon and cleanse within; Grace, grace, God's grace, Grace that is greater than all our sin.

Blessings,
Don

Daily Praise Moment

January 26

Praising Our Lord Jesus Christ Who Is The Light of the World

Isaiah 9:2 (KJV) contains a prophesy of our Lord's coming to earth:
The people who walked in darkness
Have seen a great light;
Those who dwelt in the land of the shadow of death,
Upon them a light has shined.

Where would Noah have been inside the ark if God hadn't told him to install floodlights? **He would have been in the dark!**

When I was writing this devotional a few months ago, I could see because I was wearing a battery-powered headlamp. Earlier that evening, the power went off. Everything went black. The upside of this happening was quietness – there was little sound except for the wind, blowing through the trees. That night Janet and I opened our cell phones and used the phone light to find and light candles. Its amazing how even a little bit of light can brighten a dark room.

In John 8:12 (NASB), Jesus says,
I am the Light of the world; he who follows Me will not walk in the darkness, but will have the Light of life.

As I read through the New Testament and encounter the miracles of Jesus, I'm amazed at how people sought Him out. Crowds followed Him. His Divine, life-changing Light attracted them.

Matthew 5:14-16 (NASB) records these words of Jesus:
You are the light of the world. A city that is set on a hill cannot be hidden. [15] *Nor do they light a lamp and put it under a basket, but on a lampstand, and it gives light to all who are in the house.* [16] *Let your light so shine before men, that they may see your good works and glorify your Father in heaven.*

Jesus, the Light of the world, lives in you, believer! As you consider today's Scriptures, let your musical mind hear the old hymn written by Phillip Bliss, "The Light of the World is Jesus."

The whole world was lost in the darkness of night,

The Light of the world is Jesus;
Like sunshine at noon-day His glory shone in,
The Light of the world is Jesus.
Come to the Light, 'tis shining for thee;
Sweetly the Light has dawned upon me;
Once I was blind, but now I can see:
The Light of the world is Jesus.

No darkness have we who in Jesus abide,
The Light of the world is Jesus;
We walk in the Light when we follow our Guide,
The Light of the world is Jesus.
Come to the Light, 'tis shining for thee;
Sweetly the Light has dawned upon me;
Once I was blind, but now I can see:
The Light of the world is Jesus.

Ye dwellers in darkness with sin-blinded eyes,
The Light of the world is Jesus;
Go, wash, at His bidding, and light will arise,
The Light of the world is Jesus.
Come to the Light, 'tis shining for thee;
Sweetly the Light has dawned upon me;
Once I was blind, but now I can see:
The Light of the world is Jesus.

No need of the sunlight in heaven we're told,
The Light of the world is Jesus;
The Lamb is the Light in the City of Gold,
The Light of the world is Jesus.
Come to the Light, 'tis shining for thee;
Sweetly the Light has dawned upon me;
Once I was blind, but now I can see:
The Light of the world is Jesus.

Blessings,
Don

Public Domain

Daily Praise Moment

January 27

Praising Our God Who Always Has Us on His Mind

Psalm 91:1-11 (NKJV) has these wonderful words:
1 *He who dwells in the secret place of the Most High*
Shall abide under the shadow of the Almighty.
2 *I will say of the Lord, "HE IS my refuge and my fortress;*
My God, in Him I will trust."
3 *Surely He shall deliver you from the snare of the fowler*
AND from the perilous pestilence.
4 *He shall cover you with His feathers,*
And under His wings you shall take refuge;
His truth SHALL BE YOUR shield and buckler.
5 *You shall not be afraid of the terror by night,*
NOR of the arrow THAT flies by day,
6 *NOR of the pestilence THAT walks in darkness,*
NOR of the destruction THAT lays waste at noonday.
7 *A thousand may fall at your side,*
And ten thousand at your right hand;
BUT it shall not come near you.
8 *Only with your eyes shall you look,*
And see the reward of the wicked.
9 *Because you have made the Lord, WHO IS my refuge,*
EVEN the Most High, your dwelling place,
10 *No evil shall befall you,*
Nor shall any plague come near your dwelling;
11 *For He shall give His angels charge over you,*
To keep you in all your ways.

Aren't you glad that God is always on duty, even when our brains are off!!! One of my most obvious times for having my brain turned off happened when I was installing a gas fireplace in our home. Part of the installation required replacing a small section of the gas supply line. I "turned off" the gas supply system to our home and started disassembling the pipes. As a safety check, I slightly opened the supply line valve and found that gas was still coming through the pipes. My immediate reaction was fear – gas is VERY dangerous. I quickly turned the supply line off.

Just as panic was about to kick in, my cell phone rang. The person on the phone was just calling to "check on" me – I was on his mind, and he hadn't talked with me on the phone for about two years. Prior to his retirement, my friend was head of the Maintenance Department at Tennessee School for the Deaf, and he's an expert at repairing gas, electrical and plumbing problems. I immediately asked for his advice. When I did what he said, the problem was solved, and I was able to safely finish the job.

Some people call this "coincidence" or "luck." I know better – it was "divine intervention." As a small child, someone gave me a "rabbit's foot" to bring me good luck. Somewhere in my childhood, I stopped believing in "luck" and began giving God credit for those numerous times each day when He intervenes on my behalf. I'm thankful for God's protection and blessings.

As I reflect on today's Scripture and God's provision, my musical mind begins hearing my friend, Bill Solomon, sing "When He Was on the Cross," by Ronny Hinson and Mike Payne:

I'm not on an ego trip; I'm nothing on my own.
I make mistakes, I often slip – just common flesh and bones.
But I'll prove someday just why I say I'm of a special kind –
for when He was on the cross, I was on his mind.

The look of love was on his face, thorns were on his head.
The blood was on his scarlet robe, and stained a crimson red.
Though his eyes were on the crowd that day, He looked ahead in time
for when He was on the cross, I was on his mind.

He knew me, yet He loved me. He whose glory makes the heavens
shine. So unworthy of such mercy, yet when He was on the cross,
I was on his mind.

Blessings,
Don

Daily Praise Moment

January 28

Praising Our God Who Is Conforming Us to the Image of Christ

Romans 12:1-2 (NASB), says:
1 *Therefore I urge you, brethren, by the mercies of God, to present your bodies a living and holy sacrifice, acceptable to God, which is your spiritual service of worship.* 2 *And do not be conformed to this world, but be transformed by the renewing of your mind, so that you may prove what the will of God is, that which is good and acceptable and perfect.*

We live in a culture that prides itself on making everything fit. We buy shoe inserts that can "gel" to our feet, shirts that are tapered to fit better, and my favorite – pants that have a stretch feature on the sides so they "breathe" when I need them to do so. When I eat a lot, my pants with the breathable side panels still button!!! They feel great, but if my goal is to not add to my waist size, these pants fail to give me the gentle reminder that I need when I sit down to eat!

God's plan for each of our lives is to shape us into the likeness of His Perfect Son. The world's plan is to keep us from following God's plan – to conform us to the world's culture.

I once heard a story about a reporter with very little artistic ability who was sent to interview a famous sculptor and learn the secret of his success. The sculptor had several large blocks of granite in his studio. From each piece of granite, he created a different piece of intricate artwork; artwork with exquisite detail and clarity. The sculptor was busy during the interview, so the interviewer asked, "How are you able to turn this piece of stone into such a beautiful statue of Moses?" To the question, the sculptor said, "I take my tools and simply carve away everything that doesn't look like the mighty Moses!"

This is what God is doing in our lives. On a daily basis, God is chiseling away from our lives everything that doesn't look like Christ. God's "heavenly sandpaper" is working on us so that others can see our Savior in our lives.

Romans 12:1-2, from "The Message" says:
So here's what I want you to do, God helping you: Take your everyday, ordinary life — your sleeping, eating, going-to-work, and walking-around life — and place it before God as an offering. Embracing what God does for you is the best thing you can do for him. Don't become so well-adjusted to your culture that you fit into it without even thinking. Instead, fix your attention on God. You'll be changed from the inside out. Readily recognize what he wants from you, and quickly respond to it. Unlike the culture around you, always dragging you down to its level of immaturity, God brings the best out of you, develops well-formed maturity in you.

As I meditate on today's Scriptures, my musical mind begins to hear this wonderful song, "Something Beautiful," written by Bill and Gloria Gather:

Something beautiful, something good;
All my confusion, He understood.
All I had to offer Him was brokenness and strife,
But He made something beautiful of my life.

Blessings,
Don

Heavenly Father,
Thank You for chiseling away from my life all the "stuff" that does not look like Christ. Even though it is painful at times, I know I'll be a better person when Your work is complete.

I trust You with the work You're doing in my life.

Help me have a yielded heart and help me to live out the life You give me so that when others see me, they honor You.

I love You and pray this prayer in the name that is above every name, the name of Jesus Christ.
Amen

Daily Praise Moments

January 29

Praising Our God Who Puts Believers in Our Paths to Mentor Us

Proverbs 22:6 NASB says:
[6] *Train up a child in the way he should go,*
Even when he is old he will not depart from it.

The year was 1965. My world had fallen apart. As I've shared in earlier Daily Praise moments, after graduating from high school on a Friday night, I entered East Tennessee Chest Disease Hospital on the following Monday morning because I had been diagnosed with tuberculosis. Very few of the patients who entered the hospital stayed less than six months. Some had been there for as long as seven years. My roommate who was one year older than me had already been there six weeks when I arrived. I had been promised a music scholarship to East Tennessee State University, but that dream bubble popped – it was gone.

Many people ministered to me while I was there by sending cards and letters. One of those who sent cards and letters to me regularly was Janet!!! The cards that meant the most to me were those with Scripture verses in them – verses such as these:

Matthew 21:22 (NASB)
... and all things you ask in prayer, believing, you will receive ....

Isaiah 53:5 *"But he was wounded for our transgressions, he was bruised for our iniquities: the chastisement of our peace was upon him; and* ***with his stripes we are healed****."*

I was one of the very fortunate ones – I "graduated" from the hospital in fifty (50) days, was put on limited activity for six (6) months, and in January, 1966, I enrolled in Hiwassee College.

My Dad was volunteer song leader at my home church, Corinth Baptist Church, in Loudon, Tennessee. I remember going to the church at night to read and study for school. I was a quiet, shy boy who wondered what would happen to my life.

I can remember that most nights while studying at church, I would leave the Sunday school room where I studied, go into the sanctuary, kneel in front of the pulpit and pray. I even remember one of the prayers I often prayed: "Lord, please put someone in my life who believes more than I do – someone who can help me learn to trust You more than I do."

In my first quarter in college, I took a class in Religious Studies entitled "The Teachings of Jesus." The class was taught by a very godly woman – Evelyn Laycock. God mightily used Dr. Laycock to help me. She had such a sweet, warm personality, which was what I clearly needed at that time. I remember that one of the books she had us read was "In His Steps," by Charles Sheldon – a novel about a person who faced daily challenges by asking this question before making a decision, "What would Jesus do?"

Looking back, I now see that part of my passion for trusting God with daily life came from those times. Even though I was legally an adult, in many ways I was still a child. Through the ministry of love and encouragement, I began to see that God had a wonderful plan for my life.

As I give thought to today's Scriptures and these events, my musical mind begins to hear a song written by Richard Baker and his brother, Bo Baker, entitled "His Way, Mine," which has these lyrics:

God has a place for every planned creation, a path for every star to go. He drew the course for every river's journey, now I know He has a way for me.

I place my life in the hands of God – those hands so scarred, now outstretched for me. Wherever it may be, over land, over sea, May Thy will sublime, O Thou God Divine, be mine.

Blessings,
Don

Daily Praise Moment

January 30

Praising the Holy Spirit of God Who Indwells Us

1 Corinthians 3:16 (NASB), says:
Do you not know that you are a temple of God and THAT the Spirit of God dwells in you?

Galatians 4:6 (NASB), says:
Because you are sons, God has sent forth the Spirit of His Son into our hearts, crying, 'Abba! Father!'

In yesterday's Daily Praise moment, I mentioned a book written in the late 1890's, entitled "In His Steps," by Charles Sheldon. Dr. Sheldon, who was pastor at Central Congregational Church in Topeka, Kansas, began writing one chapter of this book each week and sharing the chapter with his church on Sunday evenings. Soon, his church was packed. The storyline of the book was what happened in people's lives as they began prefacing each daily decision with the question, "What would Jesus do?"

God used this book and this question to impact many people's lives, including mine.

Believers have the Holy Spirit of God living inside us. As we yield to His leadership, He guides us into all Truth. For me, the key to hearing the Holy Spirit of God speak to me is for me to get off the throne of my life and allow Him to be in His rightful place – Lord of my life. When I yield, He leads!

As I think about it now, my heart tells me that an even better question than "What would Jesus do?" is to pray and say, "Indwelling Holy Spirit of God, what do You want me to do?"

While I meditate on today's Scripture verses, my musical mind begins to hear "Wherever He Leads, I'll Go," written by B. B. McKinney, in 1936:

"Take up thy cross and follow Me" I heard my Master say.
"I gave My life to ransom thee, surrender your all today!"
Wherever He leads, I'll go. Wherever He leads, I'll go.

I'll follow my Christ who loves me so. Wherever He leads, I'll go.

He drew me closer to His side, I sought His will to know,
And in that will I now abide, wherever He leads, I'll go
Wherever He leads, I'll go. Wherever He leads, I'll go.
I'll follow my Christ who loves me so. Wherever He leads, I'll go.

It may be thro' the shadows dim, or o'er the stormy sea,
I'll take my cross and follow Him, wherever He leadeth me.
Wherever He leads, I'll go. Wherever He leads, I'll go.
I'll follow my Christ who loves me so. Wherever He leads, I'll go.

My heart, my life, my all I bring to Christ who loves me so;
He is my Master, Lord, and King, wherever He leads I'll go.
Wherever He leads, I'll go. Wherever He leads, I'll go.
I'll follow my Christ who loves me so. Wherever He leads, I'll go.

Blessings,
Don

Public Domain

Personal Thoughts:

____

____

____

____

____

Daily Praise Moment

January 31

Praising God Who Uses Us to Train Others to Follow Him

2 Timothy 2:1-2 (NASB), says:
[1] *You therefore, my son, be strong in the grace that is in Christ*
Jesus. [2] *The things which you have heard from me in the presence of*
many witnesses, entrust these to faithful men who will be able to teach
others also.

Before Saul encountered the living Christ and had his life dramatically changed, he zealously did what he thought was work for God. He was far off base, though, killing Christians and making life miserable for those he was not able to apprehend. After his conversion, he was rejected by the "religious establishment" until Barnabas befriended him and presented him to the others as someone whose life had been changed.

Later in Paul's ministry, the young man, Timothy, learned much from Paul. God used Paul's ministry to help Timothy, just as God used Barnabas' ministry to help Paul.

Likewise, God is using you and me. We are witnesses of His on a daily basis. People assess God's character by what they see of Him in us.

One of my dear friends was Tom McKay, a United States Naval Academy graduate (in Tom's words, after graduating, he "had enough sense to join the Marine Corps!") who loved Christ and sought to serve Him on a daily basis. While all of Tom's passion for his service stemmed from the way God changed his life, some of Tom's early desire for making a difference in the lives of others could be traced back to a poem his mother made her nine children memorize before they left home. The poem, "A Bag of Tools," by RL Sharpe, has these words:

Isn't it strange how princes and kings,
And clowns that caper in sawdust rings,
And common people, like you and me
Are builders for eternity?

Each is given a bag of tools,
A shapeless mass,
A book of rules,
And each must make—
Ere life is flown—
A stumbling block
Or a stepping-stone.

As I think about today's Scripture and the mission God has given each of us, my musical mind begins to hear the lyrics of the hymn, "Reach Out and Touch," penned by Charles Brown in 1971:

Reach out and touch a soul that is hungry;
Reach out and touch a spirit in despair;
Reach out and touch a life torn and dirty,
A man who is lonely, if you care!

Reach out and touch that neighbor who hates you;
Reach out and touch that stranger who meets you;
Reach out and touch the brother who needs you;
Reach out and let the smile of God touch thro' you.

Blessings,
Don

Daily Praise Moment

February 1

Praising God Who Loves Us and Gives Us Daily Direction

Proverbs 3:5-6 (KJV) says:
5Trust in the LORD with all thine heart; and lean not unto thine own understanding. 6In all thy ways acknowledge him, and he shall direct thy paths.

In the fall of 1972, I began working as a vocational rehabilitation counselor, serving high school students at the Tennessee School for the Deaf. Deafness is a disability that not only affects hearing – it usually has a very negative effect on language development. Many students with normal intelligence struggle with language issues because they've never heard the structure of language.

My secretary, Sharon Lawson, was a strong Christian. She loved the students we served, and many of them would stop by our office as soon as the school day ended, just to say "Hi" to Ms. Sharon. One of the teenagers who stopped by each day always brought Sharon a letter expressing the joys and frustrations of her day. Each day, this student's letter began with these words:

"Dear Sharon, I am very love you, but I am very hate you."

As I think about my life, in many ways I've been saying this to God by how I've lived out my trust and commitment to Him. My ambivalence in hearing and following God is very much like I'm saying, "Dear God, I am very love You, but I am very hate You." I tell Him I love Him, but then often I only half-way follow Him. My negligence in reading His Word, sharing my faith, or listening to His still, small voice is more akin to me saying, "I am very hate You."

My prayer for me today and every day is that I will be 100-percent committed to listening to and following the leading of our Savior.

As I think on today's Scripture, my musical mind begins to hear the words of a song written by a composer who came to our church several years ago and sang -- Richard (Dick) Baker. Brother Baker wrote many wonderful songs. He is now at home with our Lord.

Last year I made contact with his daughter, and she mailed me some of her Daddy's music, which I dearly treasure. One of those songs – "All to Thee" – has these powerful words:

I have heard the voice of Jesus,
Calling clearly, "Follow Me."
No one else could ever promise
Life eternal and so free.

All to Thee, I give my all to Thee,
All to Thee, Thine only will I be;
All to Thee, O Christ of Calvary,
My prayer shall ever be, my all to Thee.

Only Jesus is the answer
For the happiness men seek;
He alone can lift life's burden,
And give strength unto the weak.

All to Thee, I give my all to Thee,
All to Thee, Thine only will I be;
All to Thee, O Christ of Calvary,
My prayer shall ever be, my all to Thee.

Blessings,
Don

Daily Praise Moment

February 2

Praising God Who Gives Us Perspective in Tough Times

1 Corinthians 13:12 (King James Version) says:
For now we see through a glass, darkly; but then face to face: now I know in part; but then shall I know even as also I am known.

The year – 1979. The place – University of Tennessee Hospital. (This is beginning to sound like a scene from a Dragnet episode – "It was a cool, spring day in Los Angeles. My partner and I were on a stakeout. My name's Friday. I'm a cop!")

My Dad and I were at UT Hospital, waiting for the right time to go upstairs in the Doctor Building and see his internist. Daddy had lung cancer. He was going through radiation treatments, and he was struggling. The treatments weren't reducing the tumor, and Daddy's chest area was so inflamed that it was hard for him to swallow.

I knew where Daddy would go when he died, but I was not ready to release him. He was so very precious to me. The spot where Dad and I were standing was perhaps 100 feet from the front entrance to the hospital. Daddy was coughing and having trouble breathing. I was beside him, looking at Dad and seeing the other doors on the sidewalk leading up to the main front door of the hospital.

A door halfway up the sidewalk opened and a woman about 35 years old came out. She looked as if she was recovering from surgery on her wrist or elbow – her arm was in a sling and bandaged. At the exact moment this woman came out the middle door, the main door of the hospital opened and a nurse wheeled a new mother outside, holding her infant. At that point, God clearly spoke to me and said, "Don, look – this is life in one snapshot. Your Daddy is nearing the end of his life; the lady coming out the middle door is half way through her life; and the young child is just getting started. Trust Me. I know best."

That day, I was given a bigger picture of life. In reality, none of us is promised tomorrow. The only day we can live is today.

As my daddy neared the end of his life, I tried to enjoy each day we had together.

In thinking about today's Scripture and the events that I've described, my musical mind begins to hear the lyrics and tune of a Bill & Gloria Gaither song – "We Have This Moment Today."

We have this moment to hold in our hand and to touch,
As it slips through our fingers like sand.
Yesterday's gone and tomorrow may never come,
But we have this moment today.

I know that my separation from my earthly father is only temporary. Someday, perhaps soon, I'll see him again. Today, though, I'm going to thank God that my Dad, Mom and brothers are with Him. Also, I'm going to tell someone who is here with me on this side of Heaven that I love them.

Blessings,
Don

PS God loves you, and I do, too.

Daily Praise Moment

February 3

Praising Our God Who Empowers Us to Be Achievers

Ecclesiastes 9:10a says:
Whatsoever thy hand findeth to do, do it with thy might....

As I think of this verse, my mind goes back to one of my heroes – a young man named Steve with whom I worked at the Tennessee School for the Deaf. Steve was profoundly deaf. He was also a thalidomide baby. Thalidomide was a sedative drug used in the 1950s and early 1960s to treat morning sickness during pregnancy. What scientists didn't know when this drug was introduced was that it could lead to very severe side effects for the babies being carried.

Steve was one of those babies. He was born with very short forearms and no thumbs on either hand. Since sign language, and particularly fingerspelling, makes use of all fingers, communicating with Steve was VERY difficult.

To deal with some of the birth defects that Steve had, he underwent multiple surgeries. Steve looked very frail compared to classmates his age. The teachers and staff coped with Steve's communication problems as best they could. All seemed to be going so-so, except for two large issues: 1. Steve wanted to play football (this didn't seem like a good idea for a young man with limited upper body strength and fragile arms/hands), and 2. Steve wanted to become a draftsman (holding a pencil and drawing all day long didn't seem like a good idea for a person without thumbs!).

Steve "pestered" the athletic director at TSD so much that the AD finally gave him a football and a kicking "tee" and told him that if he could learn to kick, he could be on the team. Steve immediately began to practice. He would be at the football field long after the other players were in the shower.

In one game, the football coach let Steve go in to attempt a field goal. Guess what? Steve kicked the field goal and TSD won the game!

The fact that this young man had done something so incredible in spite of his disabilities was picked up by the Knoxville newspapers. Soon thereafter, sports announcer Joe Garagiola talked about Steve on NPR. Then, most unexpected of all, Steve got a letter from President Nixon, congratulating him for his accomplishments.

You've probably figured out by now that Steve also became a draftsman. He worked as a draftsman for TVA for several years.

About eight years ago, I was having lunch at a small restaurant in South Knoxville and ran into a deaf man who had worked with Steve at TVA. I asked him if he knew how Steve was doing. He said that Steve was fine. In fact, he was going to be bowling with Steve (yes, bowling with a man who had no thumbs) that same night. Then he said something that really caught my attention. He said, "I don't know why, but Steve has always been one of the happiest people I've ever known."

The bottom line is that I can choose how I am going to live my life. Am I going to choose to make lemonade as Steve did? Or, am I going to decide that "life is just vanity" as Solomon was doing at the time he wrote Ecclesiastes?

As I think about today's Scripture and the memories I've shared about one of my heroes, this song, "Take My Life, Lead Me, Lord," written by R. Maines Rawls in 1969, begins to play in my head:

Take my life, lead me, Lord. Take my life, lead me, Lord.
Make my life useful to Thee.

Take my life, teach me, Lord. Take my life, teach me, Lord.
Make my life useful to Thee.

Here am I, send me, Lord. Here am I, send me, Lord.
Make my life useful to Thee.

Blessings,
Don

Daily Praise Moment

February 4

Praising God Who Empowers Us to Overcome Fears

2 Timothy 1:7 (NKJV) says:
7 *For God has not given us a spirit of fear, but of power and of love and of a sound mind.*

Several years ago Friends of Tennessee's Babies with Special Needs was having a Family Day at Natchez Trace State Park in West Tennessee. Many parents were there with their very young children who had significant developmental delays.

We had assembled a panel of adults who have disabilities to "tell their stories" to the parents. Our goal was to give a sense of hope and encouragement to these families, to help them see that the world was not coming to an end because their child had a disability.

One member of our "panel of experts" was a woman named Jamie. I introduced Jamie to the families and asked her to talk about her life experiences. She said, "Hi, My name is Jamie and I'm retarded -- but that's okay, because I know the governor!"

The tension in the room immediately died as everyone began to applaud.

Jamie was right – she did know the governor. She sat on a state disability advisory panel for the governor. She went on to say, "I work at McDonalds. I can't drive, but that's okay. I saved my money and bought a car. I hired a driver to take me where I want to go!"

Again, the parents broke into laughter and applause for the way Jamie was handling the adversities that she faced. All the speakers that day were wonderful, but Jamie "stole the show" with her bluntness and her confidence.

As believers, we might not know the governor, but we do know Someone with even more importance and power – we know the King of kings. And, we need to remember that God doesn't just want us to know ABOUT Him; He wants us to KNOW Him – to have an intimate, personal relationship with Him; a relationship where we tell Him all of our joys and sorrows. As we walk with Him, He helps us overcome fears.

As I think of today's Scripture and the story I've just shared, my musical mind begins to hear "You'll Never Walk Alone," composed by Rodgers and Hammerstein:

When you walk through the storm
Hold your head up high
And don't be afraid of the dark
At the end of the storm
There's a golden sky
And the sweet silver song of the lark

Walk on, through the wind
Walk on, through the rain
Though your dreams be tossed and blown
Walk on, walk on, with hope in your heart
And you'll never walk alone
You'll never walk alone

Walk on, walk on, with hope in your heart
And you'll never walk alone
You'll never walk alone

Blessings,
Don

Daily Praise Moment

February 5

Praising God Who Puts Godly Teachers in Our Lives

Proverbs 31: 10, 25, 26, 28a (KJV) says:
10*Who can find a virtuous woman? for her price is far above rubies.*

25*Strength and honour are her clothing; and she shall rejoice in time to come.* 26*She openeth her mouth with wisdom; and in her tongue is the law of kindness.*

28*Her children arise up, and call her blessed. ..."*

I was blessed to grow up in a home with a godly Mother. Many of you knew my Mom, and there is so much that I can and will share about her. But for today, I believe that God is leading me to write about a godly neighbor that I had – Ina Mae – who was my childhood Sunday school teacher.

Ina Mae taught a boys' Sunday school class at my church. She didn't drive and was not out in the community very much except at church; however, she had an amazing impact on the lives of many of the boys who lived in the Corinth community.

Our community was about 3 miles from Loudon, Tennessee. Houses in downtown Loudon had two or three bedrooms and a bath. Where I grew up, most houses had two bedrooms and a path. Outhouses were not the oddity – they were the norm. Ina Mae's outhouse was special, though, for two reasons: 1. it had a real toilet seat, and 2. the walls were papered with wallpaper.

Ina Mae had a big brindle dog named Wolfe. He guarded her home and provided security in our neighborhood.

Ina Mae always found ways to celebrate successes with the boys in her Sunday school class. We had wiener and marshmallow roasts, egg hunts and Christmas parties in her yard. She found ways of giving us prizes for verses memorized, and she always challenged us to learn and follow God's Word.

All of this was special, but I believe that the most special part of Ina Mae's life was the time she spent alone with God, praying for us kids and our families.

As her next door neighbor, I would often see her leave her home in the mornings, wearing a big apron and a bonnet, heading into the woods with her dog, Wolfe, to walk and talk with God. I'm convinced that the children in her class were often her topic of discussion with God, too. She knew each of us by name. We were special to her. Because we were special to her, the Bible truths that she shared with us were special to us. As I reflect on this woman's impact on my life, I'm reminded that my job as a believer is to "make disciples."

God is using each of us to impact the lives of others. My personal prayer is that our lives will count for good in the lives of others in the same way Ina Mae's life counted for good in my life and in the lives of countless other children who grew up in our community.

As I think about today's Scriptures and remember my neighbor, my musical mind begins to hear a stanza from "Worthy, You Are Worthy" written by Don Moen:

Faithful, You are faithful.
King of kings, Lord of lords,
You are faithful.

Faithful, You are faithful.
King of kings, Lord of lords,
I worship You.

Blessings,
Don

Daily Praise Moment

February 6

Praising God Who Enables Us to Succeed In Spite of Circumstances

Philippians 4:13 says:
I can do all things through Christ who strengthens me.

Philippians 4:13 is a wonderful verse that gives us such assurance that we can achieve all that God calls us to accomplish. He calls, we listen and He works through us to achieve the "things" He has called us to do.

As I meditate on this verse, my mind travels back to the early 1970s to another one of my heroes who faced tough challenges and won. Bonnie was a spunky young woman who was getting ready to graduate from Tennessee School for the Deaf, and she was determined to make it on her own.

Bonnie was in a work-study program. In addition to her academics, she had received training in food service. As a final part of her training, she entered an "on the job training" program at St. Mary's Hospital cafeteria. The nun who supervised the cafeteria was excellent, but she ran a very tight ship. I wanted to provide Bonnie with an interpreter, but the supervisor said, "No, that's not the real world. I believe Bonnie must learn to handle this." She gave Bonnie an instruction manual which was written at a higher reading level than Bonnie's teachers and I felt she could read. Then, she told Bonnie to ask for help if she needed it. With this done, she let Bonnie go into the "real world." When I checked back a few days later, the supervisor was beaming with joy. Bonnie had followed every instruction to a "T" -- all without outside help.

About five years after graduating from high school, Bonnie came back to the Homecoming Football Game, driving a brand new car that she had worked, saved and paid for herself. She was coping in spite of how the situation had looked for her. She didn't let life's challenges keep her from seeing possibilities.

The reality is that all of us are born into settings that are different. For us, the challenge is to listen to God and see our future as He sees it, not as our circumstances might try to dictate.

As I reflect on today's Scripture and remember the challenges that were in Bonnie's life, my musical mind begins to hear "Strength of the Lord," written by Phil McHugh:

Sometimes life seems like words and music
that can't quite become a song,
So we cry inside, and we try it again
and wonder what could be wrong.

But, when we turn to the Lord
at the end of ourselves
Like we've done a time or two before,
We find His truth is the same as it has always been,
We never will need more.

It's not in trying but in trusting.
It's not in running but in resting.
Not in wondering but in praying,
That we find the strength of the Lord.

Blessings,
Don

Daily Praise Moment

February 7

Praising God Who Invites Us to Come into His Presence and Rest

Matthew 11:28 – 30 (KJV) says:
Come unto me, all ye that labour and are heavy laden, and I will give you rest. Take My yoke upon you, and learn of Me; for I am meek and lowly in heart: and ye shall find rest unto your souls. For My yoke is easy, and My burden is light.

As I read through these verses, I'm transported 60 years back in time.

When I was a small child, my Dad had a quartet – The Corinth Quartet. Daddy played guitar and sang lead, or whatever part the group needed for a particular song. He was joined in this group by Lonnie Oody, Bill Thomas and Doc White. Practically every week we, along with other people from our community who loved gospel music, would meet at someone's home, share lots of food and listen as the quartet practiced. My older brother, Billy, spent the evenings with the boys who were there, but my younger brother, Larry, and I were always being carried around by the older girls. Sometimes these afternoon or evening events went on for hours.

Then, each Sunday afternoon our families would go to Lenoir City, Tennessee, to the WLIL Radio Station for a live broadcast. The quartet usually sang three or four songs, followed by a preacher giving a strong gospel sermon. The studio was VERY small. As I recall, there was seating for about 10 people. The rest of us sat on the floor and lined the walls. We were always reminded that we had to be quiet, but a hearty "Amen" was always welcomed. Daddy would strum out an opening chord on his guitar, and the quartet members would join him, leaning in together to "sing into the can" so the radio waves could carry it out "live" to all the homes in the local area.

The signature song that Daddy's quartet opened with almost every Sunday was "Come Unto Me," based on today's Scripture. As I read Matthew 11:28-30, my musical memory allows me to still clearly hear the Corinth Quartet singing these comforting words:

Hear the blessed Savior calling the oppressed,
Oh ye heavy laden, come to Me and rest.
Come, no longer tarry, I your load will bear;
Bring Me every burden, bring Me every care.

Come (oh come) unto Me (unto Me),
I (yes, I) will give you (I will give you) rest.
Take (oh take) My yoke up (take My yoke up) on you,
Hear (yes, hear) Me and be (hear Me and be) blessed.

For I (oh I) am meek and (I am meek and) lowly;
Come (oh come) and trust My might.
Come (oh come), My yoke is (come, My yoke is) easy.
Come (oh, come), My burden's light (come, My burden's light).

Blessings,
Don

Public Domain

Heavenly Father,
I thank You for giving me such a rich spiritual and musical heritage, and I pray Your best for all who read Daily Praise Moments and seek to follow our soon-coming Savior.

I pray this prayer in Jesus' name.
AMEN

Daily Praise Moment

February 8

Praising Our God Who Meets Our Needs in Tough Times

Philippians 4:19 says:
But my God shall supply all your need according to his riches in glory by Christ Jesus.

The older I get, the more convinced I am that I don't really appreciate God's blessings in my life until I'm in a crisis mode. As various crises have happened in my life, God has dramatically intervened. Maybe this is where the phrase "no pain, no gain" originated!!!

One crisis that comes to mind as I meditate on today's Scripture happened when I was 15 years old. Before I was born, Daddy had a hunting accident that left him with a bad limp. Miraculously, he survived a gunshot wound that could easily have taken his life, but that is another day's story.

In the fall of 1962, Dad began having very serious problems with his leg that had been injured in the hunting accident. He developed an infection in his knee that could easily have resulted in an amputation. The doctor was successful in saving Dad's life and his leg, but the only recourse at that time was to stiffen his knee. Dad went into a coma for about a week, and Dr. Bagwell who was treating him was not sure if Dad would survive. We prayed hard for him to live, and God answered.

Dad came home from the hospital after about three weeks, but his level of health was such that Mom had to take a "leave of absence" from the hosiery mill where she worked to take care of him. We were most blessed that Dad survived, but with both parents out of work, our family resources became VERY tight. It was almost Thanksgiving, and we were scrimping by to have food to eat.

Then, the day before Thanksgiving, the pastor of our church, Joe Caldwell, came walking down the road from his house to ours. That wasn't unusual, but that day, what Brother Joe was doing WAS UNUSUAL.

Preacher Caldwell was leading a turkey down the road from his house to ours. He had a twine string tied around the turkey's leg, and he walked it to our home.

Brother Joe "sacrificed" the turkey, hung it on a tree in our yard and "dry picked" it. A cloud of feathers from the suspended bird was flying all around him. It truly was a sight to behold!!!

We had a wonderful Thanksgiving that year – one that I'll never forget. Soon thereafter, our church gave us a "food pounding" and we had plenty of food to help us until Mom was able to go back to work.

As I give thought to today's Scripture and the incident that I've related to you, my musical mind begins to hear a words from a hymn, "Just When I Need Him Most," penned by William C. Poole in 1907 and put to a Charles H. Gabriel tune that was written that same year:

Just when I need Him, Jesus is near
Just when I falter, just when I fear
Ready to help me, ready to cheer
Just when I need Him most.

Just when I need Him most
Just when I need Him most
Jesus is near to comfort and cheer
Just when I need Him most.

Blessings,
Don

Daily Praise Moment

February 9

Praising Our Savior Who Gave His Life to Protect Us

Psalm 91:1-4 (NKJV) says:
1 *He who dwells in the secret place of the Most High*
Shall abide under the shadow of the Almighty.
2 *I will say of the Lord, "HE IS my refuge and my fortress;*
My God, in Him I will trust."
3 *Surely He shall deliver you from the snare of the fowler*
AND from the perilous pestilence.
4 *He shall cover you with His feathers,*
And under His wings you shall take refuge;
His truth SHALL BE YOUR shield and buckler.

When I was in elementary school, I joined the 4-H Club. My 4-H Club project was chickens. Most of the chickens I raised were Rhode Island Reds. One of our friends raised game chickens and took them to chicken fights, but that's another story.

We never raised fighting chickens, but we did have a few game chickens in our flock. Game chickens had their own built-in camouflage system. Out in the woods, they could sit down and be almost impossible to spot, since their feathers blended so well. Rather than use the chicken house as their place to lay eggs, the game hens usually built their nests in the woods. If you did not find the nest, the hen would lay her eggs and begin the "setting" process, preparing to raise little chicks.

Once the little chicks hatched, it was very dangerous to come near them or the mother hen. On a calm day, the chicks would be searching for food, maybe two to four feet from their mother. If a potential predator came toward the baby chicks, the hen would begin clucking and all her babies would scurry back to her, snuggling as close to her as possible. She would then sit down on them – all her chicks would be safely under her wings.

If someone made the mistake of walking up to her, she would fly straight for the person's face, attacking them with all her might. She was willing to sacrifice her own life to protect her little ones.

Aren't you glad that the Lord Jesus Christ covers us with the shelter of His wings, keeping us safe.

As I meditate on today's Scripture, my musical mind begins to hear Chris Tomlin sing "Shout to the Lord," written by Darlene Zschech:

My Jesus, My Savior,
Lord, there is none like You;
All of my days I want to praise
The wonders of Your mighty love.

My comfort, my shelter,
Tower of refuge and strength;
Let every breath, all that I am
Never cease to worship You.

Shout to the Lord, all the earth, Let us sing
Power and majesty, praise to the King;
Mountains bow down and the seas will roar
At the sound of Your name.

I sing for joy at the work of Your hands,
Forever I'll love You, forever I'll stand,
Nothing compares to the promise I have in You.
Nothing compares to the promise I have in You.

Blessings,
Don

PS We, as believers, are under the shelter of the Almighty, and we have a wonderful reason to "Shout to the Lord."

Daily Praise Moment

February 10

Praising Our God Who Reveals Himself to Us through His Son, Jesus Christ

John 14:8-9 (NKJV) records this scene:
8 *Philip said to Him, "Lord, show us the Father, and it is sufficient for us."*

9 *Jesus said to him, "Have I been with you so long, and yet you have not known Me, Philip? He who has seen Me has seen the Father; so how can you say, 'Show us the Father'?"*

In the "Fifth Discipline Field Book," by Peter Senge and Associates, there is information about a tribe in the South African region of Natal where the people greet one another with the phrase, "Sawu bona," which means, "I see you." The response that the person spoken to gives back is, "Sikhona," or "I am here." The implication is that in that culture, until a person is seen by others, that person doesn't exist!

Before I jump to the conclusion that these people have a limited understanding of life, I'm reminded that God is ALWAYS with us, but until we "see" Him in our lives, we severely limit His freedom to work in us and through us. Conversely, as we acknowledge His presence, He moves mightily in us and through us, touching and changing not only us, but also those with whom we have contact.

"Seeing" God in our lives often stems from a strong inner desire – As I WANT to see Him, He reveals Himself to me.

As I consider today's Scriptures, two songs begin to be played in my musical mind, "Open Our Eyes, Lord" by Robert Cull (first verse), and "Come into His Presence" by Lynn Baird (second verse):

Open our eyes, Lord, we want to see Jesus,
To reach out and touch Him and say that we love Him.

Open our ears, Lord, and help us to listen.
Open our eyes, Lord, we want to see Jesus.

Come into His presence with thanksgiving in your heart
and give Him praise, and give Him praise.

Come into His presence with thanksgiving in your heart,
your voices raise, your voices raise.

Give glory and honor and power unto Him,
Jesus, the name above all names.

Blessings,
Don

Heavenly Father,
We acknowledge Your presence in our lives today, lifting up praises to You in the strong and mighty name of Your Son, the Lord Jesus Christ.
AMEN

Daily Praise Moment

February 11

Praising God Who Calls Us to Minister to Others

John 13:13-15 (NKJV) records Jesus as He teaches His disciples: *"13 You call Me Teacher and Lord, and you say well, for so I am. 14 If I then, your Lord and Teacher, have washed your feet, you also ought to wash one another's feet. 15 For I have given you an example that you should do as I have done to you."*

Jesus wants more than just mental assent to His teachings – He wants real followers who willingly and joyfully serve others.

Several years ago, my wife, Janet, and I heard a motivational speaker who was also a strong Christian. He was talking about the importance of following Jesus Christ, of giving Him first place in your life. In the course of his presentation, he told a story of a young man from his church talking to an older man. Here's how the conversation went:

The young man said to the elderly man, "I'm going into the ministry!"
The elderly man said, "You're what?"
The young man said, "I'm going into the ministry!"
The elderly man said, "You're what?"
The young man, thinking that the older man must not have heard him, shouted, "I'M GOING INTO THE MINISTRY!"
The elderly man then said, "What are you in now?"
The young man said, "Well, nothing, but I'm going into the ministry!"
The elderly man said, "Son, if you're not IN the ministry when you GO IN the ministry, you WON'T BE in the ministry when you GET IN the ministry!"

I believe that God has ministry roles for all believers to play -- all believers are called to minister.

As I meditate on today's Scriptures and reflect on the story I've shared, my musical mind begins to hear Larnelle Harris singing "I Give All My Life To You," which God inspired him to write:

I give all my service to You,
I give all my service to You.
No matter the cost, or what others do,
I give all my service to You.

I give all my problems to You,
I give all my problems to You.
No matter the cost, or what others do,
I give all my problems to You.

I give all my family to You,
I give all my family to You.
No matter the cost, or what others do,
I give all my family to You.

I give all my future to You,
I give all my future to You.
No matter the cost, or what others do,
I give all my future to You.

I give all my worship to You,
I give all my worship to You.
No matter the cost, or what others do,
I give all my worship to You.

I give all my worship to You.

Blessings,
Don

Daily Praise Moment

February 12

Praising Our God Who Loves Us and Rescues Us

Psalm 127:3 (NASB) says:
Behold, children are a gift of the LORD,
The fruit of the womb is a reward.

As I've shared in earlier Daily Praise Moments, a few years ago God burdened me to speak to parents of very young children. The task He gave me was to compliment the baby and say, "Children are a gift of the Lord." Most parents agree and seem pleased. My hope and prayer is that those who do not see their child as a treasure that God has entrusted to them will give thought to the comment and begin to value the gift they've been given.

I was blessed to be born into a home where all the children were cherished. However, sometimes cherishing your children means being stretched beyond your "comfort zone."

As I think this thought, my mind immediately races back 60 years to Citico, a small mountain community on the Little Tennessee River in East Tennessee.

One of the activities daddy loved was taking our family (and anyone else who would go) to Citico. We always went to Rigsby's Store and availed ourselves of the swimming area across the road from the store. Mom planned the food and made sure we had dry clothes. Another one of Mom's jobs was calling Larry and me out of the water about every hour and helping us warm up – letting our lips change back to red instead of the shivering blue they had changed to from being in the cold water too long. Though Bill got cold, too, he was considered old enough to make his own decisions. Daddy loved the water and he taught us boys to love it, too.

Momma never learned to swim. Her idea of living dangerously was wading in ankle deep water. The only time I ever remember seeing Momma in water more than knee deep was a day when Larry stretched mom out of her "comfort zone." He was about 4 years old. He had watched older kids run down the slope, jump into the river and swim away safely. The place they jumped was too deep for Larry – it was over his head, and he hadn't yet learned to swim. Daddy and most of the other swimmers were on the other side of the river. When momma saw Larry jump in the river, she didn't hesitate – she did what you would expect – she jumped into the river and saved his life!

As believers, God wants us to value others the way momma valued Larry. We must get out of our "comfort zones" and help others escape from the dangerous paths they are traveling; paths that are leading them away from the One who gave His life so all who will trust Him can have a life-changing relationship with Almighty God.

As I think about today's Scripture and the scene I've just described, my musical mind begins to hear an old gospel song, "Rescue the Perishing," penned by Fanny Crosby in 1869:

Rescue the perishing, care for the dying, snatch them in pity from sin and the grave; weep o'er the erring one, lift up the fallen, tell them of Jesus, the mighty to save. Rescue the perishing, care for the dying, Jesus is merciful, Jesus will save.

Though they are slighting Him, still He is waiting, waiting the penitent child to receive; plead with them earnestly, plead with them gently; He will forgive if they only believe. Rescue the perishing, care for the dying, Jesus is merciful, Jesus will save.

Down in the human heart, crushed by the tempter, feelings lie buried that grace can restore; touched by a loving heart, wakened by kindness, chords that were broken will vibrate once more. Rescue the perishing, care for the dying, Jesus is merciful, Jesus will save.

Rescue the perishing, duty demands it; strength for thy labor the Lord will provide; back to the narrow way patiently win them; Tell the poor wand'rer a Savior has died. Rescue the perishing, care for the dying, Jesus is merciful, Jesus will save.

Blessings,
Don

Daily Praise Moment

February 13

Praising Our God Who Is Always Faithful

2 Corinthians 1:20 (HCSB) says:
For every one of God's promises is "Yes" in Him. Therefore the "Amen" is also through Him for God's glory through us..

Another verse that communicates this great truth is 1 Thessalonians 5:24 (NASB), which says:
Faithful is He who calls you, and He also will bring it to pass.

God is our Faithful and True God. He calls us to be of service for Him, and He empowers us to accomplish the tasks that He calls us to perform. And, whether we know it or not, we are influencing others by the way we live out our spiritual lives.

I've had lots of spiritual mentors in my life – people who have helped me in my spiritual walk. At different stages in my life's journey, these folks have been sent by God into my world.

Some are heroes because they encouraged me to be more trusting of our Heavenly Father. Others have been notable examples of a life trait that God wanted me to have. Some were folks who called my mistakes to my attention. All have added to my spiritual walk as I've heard their words and observed the deeds they've lived out.

One person whose impact on my life is being remembered today is David Russell. David was a quiet man who went home to Heaven a few years ago. Most of the impact he made on me was the result of his actions, not his words.

When David was a very young child, he was struck by a car while crossing Chapman Highway in Knoxville. Thank God, he survived, but he was left with severe disabilities that he coped with for the rest of his life. Walking was a major challenge – he dragged one of his legs and was constantly wearing out shoes. One of his arms was also badly damaged.

Sometimes David would have "spasms" with his arm, making it a challenge for him to control its movement. Two things were never problems for David, though: (1) his commitment to faithfulness to his Lord and His church; and (2) having a positive attitude toward life. Being in church was paramount to David, and he always greeted others with a warm, caring smile.

On several occasions, David and I visited church prospects together. Though he always said very little, I'm sure the impact that his visit made was always greater than mine. One of the families we visited lived on a small hillside with a gravel driveway. Seeing David struggle to make the visit – that was enough to let the people know that he loved his Lord and wanted them to know Him, too.

As I think of today's Scripture and the example of faithfulness that my friend, David, lived, my musical mind begins to hear the song, "You're the Only Jesus," by Gordon Jensen, which has these challenging lyrics:

If not in you, I wonder where will they ever see the One who really cares? If not from you, how will they find, there's One who heals the broken heart, and gives sight to the blind?

You're the only Jesus that some will ever see. And you're the only words of life, some will ever read, so let them see in you the One in whom is all they'll ever need, 'cause you're the only Jesus, some will ever see.

And if not you, I wonder who, will show them love, and love alone can make things new? If not from you, how will they learn, there's one who'll trade their hopelessness and give joy in return?

You're the only Jesus that some will ever see. And you're the only words of life, some will ever read, so let them see in you the One in whom is all they'll ever need, 'cause you're the only Jesus, some will ever see.

Blessings,
Don

Daily Praise Moment

February 14

Praising Our God Who Is LOVE and Who Loves Us with An Everlasting LOVE

1 Corinthians 13:1-8 (NKJV) has these inspiring words:
1 *Though I speak with the tongues of men and of angels, but have not love, I have become sounding brass or a clanging cymbal.* 2 *And though I have the gift of prophecy, and understand all mysteries and all knowledge, and though I have all faith, so that I could remove mountains, but have not love, I am nothing.* 3 *And though I bestow all my goods to feed the poor, and though I give my body to be burned, but have not love, it profits me nothing.*

4 *Love suffers long and is kind; love does not envy; love does not parade itself, is not puffed up;* 5 *does not behave rudely, does not seek its own, is not provoked, thinks no evil;* 6 *does not rejoice in iniquity, but rejoices in the truth;* 7 *bears all things, believes all things, hopes all things, endures all things.* 8 *Love never fails."*

Romans 8:38-39 (NKJV) says:
38 *For I am persuaded that neither death nor life, nor angels nor principalities nor powers, nor things present nor things to come,* 39 *nor height nor depth, nor any other created thing, shall be able to separate us from the love of God which is in Christ Jesus our Lord.*

Guys, it's VALENTINE'S DAY. What a great day to appreciate your "special someone."

Many years ago I was asked to speak at a young couples retreat. The theme was "LOVE." As we began, I gave the couples these two scenarios to consider: "Imagine yourself and your sweetheart, walking barefoot on a quiet beach. The gentle breeze and the filtered light of sunset accent the striking features in your sweetheart's face. Your feelings are running rampant. Do you feel it?" Then I asked, "Is this love?" All of the couples said, "YES!!!"

Then, I painted a second scene: "You've had a hard day at work. You arrive home, expecting a quiet, restful evening. You open the door, and find a dog that needs walking, toys and dirty clothes on the floor, and you hear your wife in the restroom, 'driving the porcelain bus.' Is it LOVE you're feeling?" Many said, "NO."

While love is often associated with feelings, TRUE LOVE IS A DECISION! LOVE is choice we make. There is no greater role model for love than our SAVIOR. HE loves us whether we're "up and out" or "down and out." Sometimes, we question whether anyone could or would want to love us, but the truth is – WE ARE LOVED!!! OUR SAVIOR is calling us to rest in HIS LOVE, to yield ourselves to HIS LOVE, and to give our LOVING SAVIOR complete control of ourselves to HIM. It is only when we surrender to HIS loving control that we fully experience HIS loving care.

As I think of today's Scripture, my musical mind begins to hear "I Am Loved," penned by Bill and Gloria Gaither:

I am loved, I am loved, I can risk loving you, for the One who knows me best, loves me most. I am loved, you are loved, won't you please take my hand. We are free to love each other, we are loved.

I said, "If You knew, You wouldn't want me. My scars are hidden by the face I wear." He said, "My child, my scars go deeper, and it was love for you that put them there."

I am loved, I am loved, I can risk loving you, for the One who knows me best, loves me most. I am loved, you are loved, won't you please take my hand. We are free to love each other, we are loved.

Forgiven, I repeat it, I'm forgiven, and clean before my Lord I freely stand. Forgiven, I can dare forgive my brother. Forgiven, I reach out to take your hand.

I am loved, I am loved, I can risk loving you, for the One who knows me best, loves me most. I am loved, you are loved, won't you please take my hand. We are free to love each other, we are loved.

Blessings,
Don

Daily Praise Moment

February 15

Daily Praise Moment

Praising God for People in Who Inspire Us and Pray for Us

2 Timothy 2:15 (NKJV) has these words:
Be diligent to present yourself approved to God, a worker who does not need to be ashamed, rightly dividing the word of truth.

Many years ago as our church was preparing for revival, I was asked to lead a "cottage prayer meeting" with one of our elderly, quiet saints, Mrs. Crosha Smith. Crosha was blind and had severe spinal issues that made mobility hard – she rarely left home.

I began our time by reading Scriptures on the importance of prayer, shared a few comments and led the group in praying for the people and situations that concerned them. I was feeling pretty good about what I had done, in fact you could say I was proud of how it had gone. When I turned the session over to Crosha's time, this humble saint of God made a comment on prayer, then said something like this: "Over in 1 Samuel, chapter __, it says ...." Then, she quoted an entire chapter from 1 Samuel. Then, she made another comment and quoted another entire chapter from a different Old Testament book. This occurred about three or four times before she decided that it was time to pray. Her intention in doing this was not aimed at my pride – she was just sharing her heart with us, letting us know that there were clear examples in Scripture where people had earnestly prayed and God had miraculously intervened.

About a year later, I visited Crosha with David Williams, a friend who was getting ready to move to Dallas/Ft. Worth to attend seminary. We had a wonderful visit with Crosha and before we left, we asked her to remember us in her prayers. About two years later, I was checking on some of our elderly church members and dropped by to visit Crosha. Again, we had a wonderful time together. Just before I left, I asked Crosha if she would pray for me. As soon as I made this request, I noticed that her whole personality changed.

Even before she said a word, I could see on her face that she was suddenly very sad. I asked her what was wrong. She said, "You just asked me to remember you in my prayers. About two years ago, you were here with that young man, David Williams, who was going off to seminary, and you asked me to pray for both of you. I've been praying daily for both of you since you asked!"

Suddenly, the light came on for me! Much of what had been going right in my life was not because of what I had done – it was due to the prayers made on my behalf by God's quiet saints! Crosha Smith had been living out Colossians 1:3, where the Apostle Paul says to the Colossian church, *"3 We give thanks to the God and Father of our Lord Jesus Christ, praying always for you."*

As I think about today's Scripture and the incidents I've just shared, my musical mind begins to hear lyrics from "Somebody's Praying Me Through," by Darrell R Brown and Ty Lacy:

Pressing over me like a big blue sky, I know someone has me on their heart tonight. That's why I know it's gonna be alright, 'cause somebody's praying me through, somebody's praying me through.

It may be my Mother, it might be my Dad, or an old friend I've forgot I had, but whoever it is I'm so glad that; Somebody's praying me through, Somebody's praying me through.

Through the tears, through the rain, through the sorrow, through the pain it keeps bringing me through over and over again.

So when you're drowning in a sea of hurt and it feels like life couldn't get any worse, there's a blessing waiting to push back the curse, 'cause somebody's praying you through, somebody's praying you through.

Blessings,
Don

Daily Praise Moment

February 16

Praising Our God Who Empowers Us to Live Fruitful Lives

Galatians 5:22-23 (NKJV) says:
But the fruit of the Spirit is love, joy, peace, longsuffering, kindness, goodness, faithfulness, 23 *gentleness, self-control. Against such there is no law.*

I've always been intrigued with this passage. One of the first things that has been hard for me to grasp is that this Scripture does not say "fruits." It says "fruit."

The mental image that emerges in my head as I think about the fruit of the Spirit is a cluster of grapes, with the different grapes having different names on them. There is a "love" grape and a "joy" grape, etc., all in the same cluster.

The second thing that jumps out at me is that this passage **does NOT** say that these are Don's fruit. **The fruit is produced by God's Holy Spirit, who lives inside all of us who are true believers. He produces the fruit.**

The third thing that I think is important about this passage is that God's Holy Spirit, or the Spirit of Jesus Christ, doesn't give us lots of the "love" part of the fruit, but none of the self-control part of the fruit – the fruit of the Spirit is a complete cluster. Could it be that we don't always practice the longsuffering, or patience, part of the fruit because we don't really know that we have that fruit?

A companion passage is John 15:5, where Jesus says:
"I am the vine, you are the branches. He who abides in Me, and I in him, bears much fruit; for without Me you can do nothing."

Our job as believers is to abide in **the Vine** (the **Lord Jesus Christ**); as we do, **He** produces the fruit. Grunting and straining can't help me produce fruit. Fruit (love, joy, peace, patience, goodness, faithfulness, gentleness and self-control) is produced when I (the branch) yield control to **the Vine** – when I recognize that I can't, but **He** can, and I yield to **His** control.

As I meditate on today's verses, my musical mind begins to hear "His Strengh Is Perfect, by Jerry Salley and Steven Curtis Chapman:

I can do all things Through Christ who gives me strength,
But sometimes I wonder what He can do through me.
No great success to show. No glory on my own,
Yet in my weakness He is there to let me know.

His strength is perfect when our strength is gone.
He'll carry us when we can't carry on.
Raised in his power the weak become strong.
His strength is perfect. His strength is perfect.

Blessings,
Don

Lord Jesus,
Thank You for gifting me with the fruit of the Spirit.

Forgive me for those times when I stubbornly hang on to "my way" when You are wanting Peace and Patience to shine from my life.

Forgive me when I feel offended when You're wanting me to allow Goodness and Kindness to be seen.

Forgive me for those times when I'm pressing on, when You want Self Control to be evident. Help me realize that my true job is to abide in You and allow Your character to shine forth.

I love You and I want to love You more.
Amen

Daily Praise Moment

February 17

Praising Our God Who Restores Us When We Fall

John 21:15-17 says:
15 So when they had finished breakfast, Jesus said to Simon Peter, "Simon, son of John, do you love Me more than these?" He said to Him, "Yes, Lord; You know that I love You." He said to him, "Tend My lambs." 16 He said to him again a second time, "Simon, son of John, do you love Me?" He said to Him, "Yes, Lord; You know that I love You." He said to him, "Shepherd My sheep." 17 He said to him the third time, "Simon, son of John, do you love Me?" Peter was grieved because He said to him the third time, "Do you love Me?" And he said to Him, "Lord, You know all things; You know that I love You." Jesus said to him, "Tend My sheep.?"

Simon (whose name Jesus changed to Peter) had been the "gung ho" disciple who was always out front, following Jesus. Remember the time when Jesus asked him who others said Jesus was? Simon said, "Some say you're a prophet – a holy man." Then, Jesus said, "Simon, Who do you say I am?" Simon's response was, "You are the Christ, the Son of the Living God." At that point, Jesus gave Simon a new name, "Peter," or "the Rock," and Jesus said that on this confession – this acknowledgement that He is God incarnate, He would build His church.

The interchange described in John 21:15-17 occurred AFTER Jesus was crucified. In fact, this was the third encounter Jesus had with His disciples after His resurrection. Simon Peter, the "gung ho" follower who acknowledged Jesus being the Son of God, on three occasions during the night of Jesus' "trials" prior to His crucifixion, denied being a follower of Jesus, even saying that he did not know Jesus. In his shame, Simon Peter, whom Jesus challenged to leave his nets and fish for men, had gone back to just fishin'. And now, Jesus is giving Peter a chance to express his love for Christ and to renew his commitment to truly follow Him.

Our definition of the word, "love," just doesn't capture the significance of what is said in these verses. On the first and second times when

Jesus asked Simon Peter if he loved him, Jesus used the word "agapao." In essence, Jesus said, "Simon, do you love me with a sacrificial, whole hearted love; a love that is greater than your love for the boats, the fish, and your friends?"

Instead of answering, "Yes, I love you with a whole-hearted, sacrificial kind of love," Simon said, "I love you as a friend" to both of Jesus' first two questions.

The third time, Jesus said to Simon, "Do you love Me as a friend (phileo)," and Simon said, "Yes, I love you as a friend."

Jesus meets us at our point of need. He wants us to follow Him with our whole heart, and He shepherds us along, teaching us to trust Him more as we walk with Him. In John 15:14, Jesus said, *"You are My friends if you do whatever I command you."* As we confess our sins, He forgives and restores our relationship with Him.

As I mull (i.e., deeply consider, chew on) today's Scriptures, my musical mind begins to hear some of the lyrics of a song God inspired me to write several years ago:

I look into Your eyes, and find, to my surprise,
Instead of condemnation, Love looks back at me.
And now I realize that all of Satan's lies
Were meant to keep me bound to him, but now I'm free.

Blessings,
Don

PS The day I wrote this Daily Praise Moment was President's Day. God's Holy Spirit spoke to me that day asking me, "Is Jesus the President of your life, Don, or are you only allowing Him to be a Resident in your life?" God's Holy Spirit was reminding me that the control center of my life must be constantly yielded to the One who made me and has my best interests in His heart. After all, He is LORD. My job is servant!

Daily Praise Moment

February 18

Praising Our God Who Is Always Faithful

1 Corinthians 1:9 (NIV) says:
God, who has called you into fellowship with his Son Jesus Christ our Lord, is faithful.

As a child in the community where I grew up, a handshake was considered a bond. People sold property, traded cars, swapped dogs, and made loans based on a handshake. If a promise was made, the promised action occurred.

Maybe it was just the rural culture where I lived, but as much as people enjoyed daily accomplishments, most people looked forward to a brighter day ahead. Heaven was considered a real place – a place where the "trials of this life" would be over.

One of the popular songs that was heard in more places than just church had these lyrics:

This world is not my home, I'm just a-passin' through.
My treasures are laid up somewhere beyond the blue.
The angels beckon me from Heaven's open door,
and I can't feel at home in this world anymore.

O Lord, You know I have no friend like You.
If Heaven's not my home, then Lord, what will I do?
The angels beckon me from Heaven's open door,
and I can't feel at home in this world anymore.

The reality is that God meets our needs as we trust Him. Paul, in Philippians 4:11b-13 (NASB) said:
"... for I have learned to be content in whatever circumstances I am.
12 I know how to get along with humble means, and I also know how to live in prosperity; in any and every circumstance I have learned the secret of being filled and going hungry, both of having abundance and suffering need. 13 I can do all things through Him who strengthens me."

Again, perhaps it was the local community where I grew up, but there was a culture of concern. People took care of each other; they were faithful to God and to one another. And while some people obviously fared better than others in the accumulation of possessions, there was definitely not a need for a "Whoever Dies with The Most Toys Wins" bumper sticker. God had a much higher priority in people's lives as a group than He seems to enjoy in the culture that we live in today.

As I think about today's Scripture verses, my musical mind begins to hear "Only One Life," written by Lanny Wolfe:

It matters so little how much you may own,
the places you've been or the people you've known,
for it all comes to nothing when placed at His feet.
It's nothing to Jesus, just memories to keep.

Only one life, so soon it will pass.
Only what's done for Christ will last.
Only one chance to do His will,
so give to Jesus all your days;
it's the only life that pays, when you recall,
you have but one life.

Blessings,
Don

PS Remember, friend, that as much as significant people in your life love you, God loves you more!

Daily Praise Moment

February 19

Praising Our God Who Gives Us Principles to Follow for Our Good

Proverbs 22:28 (NKJV) says:
Do not remove the ancient landmark which your fathers have set.

The world we live in today differs greatly from the one I grew up in. Today, many homes have built-in security systems. Thieves still find ways of stealing, even when the homes have electronic safety systems.

When I was a child, some stealing occurred, but it was rare. I remember an incident from my childhood that shows the contrast.

Our family was getting ready to go to camping. Something had occurred that gave my Dad concern that I hadn't seen before. He turned to Mom and said, "With all that is happening, I think we need to lock the house!" Mom agreed.

We proceeded to pack up the car with the camping gear, then Mom came back to report a problem. She couldn't find the key to the house! Mom and Dad hadn't locked the house in such a long time that neither of them had any idea about where to look for the key. Granted, our family didn't have many things others might want, but still – we didn't know where to look for the key!

One of the basic principles that God gives us to live by is honesty. We see evidence of God's landmark of honesty in the Ten Commandments. Commandment 8 says, "Do Not Steal" and Commandment 10 says, "Do Not Covet." It isn't that God doesn't want us to have stuff – He just wants us to receive it honestly. And, as we depend on Him for what we need, He meets our needs without our having to steal from others. After all, He is Jehovah–Jireh, the Lord Who Provides.

As I think of today's Scripture, my musical mind begins to hear "Take Time to Be Holy," written in the late 1800s by William Longstaff and George Stebbins:

Take time to be holy, speak oft with thy Lord;
Abide in Him always, and feed on His Word.
Make friends of God's children, help those who are weak,
Forgetting in nothing His blessing to seek.

Take time to be holy, the world rushes on;
Spend much time in secret with Jesus alone –
By looking to Jesus, like Him thou shalt be;
Thy friends in thy conduct, His likeness shall see.

Take time to be holy, let Him be thy Guide,
And run not before Him, whatever betide;
In joy or in sorrow, still follow thy Lord,
And, looking to Jesus, still trust in His Word.

Take time to be holy, be calm in thy soul;
Each thought and each motive beneath His control;
Thus led by His Spirit to fountains of love,
Thou soon shalt be fitted for service above.

Blessings,
Don

Daily Praise Moment

February 20

Praising Our God Who Is Trustworthy

Isaiah 26:3-4 says:
3 *You will keep in perfect peace*
those whose minds are steadfast,
because they trust in You.
4 *Trust in the LORD forever,*
for the LORD, the LORD himself, is the Rock eternal.

Several years ago, we were driving in Des Moines, Iowa, near Drake University, when we passed a gas station which had this sign over the pumps, "In God We Trust – All Others Pay Cash." Sometimes others aren't trustworthy, but God ALWAYS is. He wants us to trust Him, not only with our eternal security, but also with our daily needs. As we learn to trust Him with our today and our tomorrows, He can build generosity into our character.

With our economy in the shape it is in, many people are having severe hardships. As believers, God wants us to be good stewards of the resources He has entrusted to us. And, He wants us to remember that our resources aren't really ours; they are His, since we (and everything we own) belong to Him. As He leads us, He can use the resources He has given us to accomplish His goals.

With the health issues that I've faced in my lifetime, I've often thought about how life can be much shorter than we want it to be. One major lesson that I've learned, though, is this: **Ownership Is A Myth**. After such a sobering thought, a light-hearted story may add levity to how we're feeling, so here goes!

The setting for the story was shortly after one of America's richest men passed away. People were talking. One person said to his friend, "I wonder how much old What's-His-Name left?" His friend turned to him and said, "I know exactly how much he left! He left it ALL!" And, truly that is what we're going to do at some future date, so it is important that we lay up treasures in Heaven!

God wants us to be hilarious givers – giving as He leads us to give. Personally, I believe that God wants us as believers to generously support our churches where the Truth is preached. I believe that my tithe should come first, even before taxes are computed. I also believe that God wants me to be open to support other causes that He leads me to support. As we give this way, God's supply line to us is open, and He meets our needs. Luke 6:38 says, *Give and it shall be given unto you. A good measure, pressed down, shaken together and running over, will be poured into your lap. For with the measure you use, it will be measured to you.*

As I think of today's verses, my musical mind begins to hear "There Is A River," by David and Max Sapp, which has these lyrics:

There is a river, and it flows from deep within
There is a fountain, that frees the soul from sin
Come to this water; there is a vast supply
There is a river, that never shall run dry

There was a thirsty woman,
She was drawing from a well.
Her life was ruined and wasted
And her soul was bound for hell.
Oh but then she met the master
And he told about her sin,
And he said "if you drink this water,
You'll never thirst again."

There is a river, and it flows from deep within.
There is a fountain that frees the soul from sin.
Come to this water; there is a vast supply.
There is a river that never shall run dry.

Blessings,
Don

Daily Praise Moment

February 21

Praising God Who Equips and Strengthens Us for Spiritual Battle (Part 1)

Ephesians 6:10-18 (NASB) says:
Finally, be strong in the Lord and in the strength of His might. [11] *Put on the full armor of God, so that you will be able to stand firm against the schemes of the devil.* [12] *For our struggle is not against flesh and blood, but against the rulers, against the powers, against the world forces of this darkness, against the spiritual forces of wickedness in the heavenly places.* [13] *Therefore, take up the full armor of God, so that you will be able to resist in the evil day, and having done everything, to stand firm.*

As believers, we face a very real battle – a spiritual battle. The enemy, Satan, seeks our destruction, while our Lord Jesus Christ has our protection and well-being in His heart.

Consider these words of our Lord, recorded in John 10:10
"The thief comes only to steal and kill and destroy; I came that they may have life, and have it abundantly."

I believe that the "thief" is Satan himself. He uses all kinds of arguments to keep us from recognizing the real battle. He knows that the more we know we are at war with him and his demons, the more likely we are to trust our Savior with the outcome. Often, Satan will say these kinds of things to us: "Nobody believes in the devil except idiots," or "You're smarter than this – only a really naïve person would believe such foolery."

If Satan sees that we're starting to see the reality of the warfare we're in, then he changes his tactics and seeks to make us too fearful of him to engage in combat. He wants us to see him like David's brothers and all the other soldiers of Israel saw Goliath. He tells us things like, "There's no way you're going to win this battle. I'm much too strong for you."

And, the reality is, without the Lord Jesus Christ living in us and having His rightful place as Lord on the leadership throne of our lives, we are not equipped for spiritual battle.

Without Christ, we're like the little boy who wanted a pony for Christmas, but only got a stick horse. When his friend asked him how he liked his stick horse, the little boy said, "Real cowboys have real horses, but I have to do my own galloping!"

Fortunately, though, as believers, we have God's Holy Spirit living inside us. As we give Him control of our lives, He gives us the power and strength to stand firm and to overcome the enemy.

As I think of today's Scripture, my musical mind begins to hear "The Battle Belongs to the Lord," penned by Jamie Owens-Collins:

In heavenly armor, we enter the land,
The battle belongs to the Lord.
No weapon that's fashioned against us shall stand.
The battle belongs to the Lord.
We sing glory, honor, power and strength to the Lord.
We sing glory, honor, power and strength to the Lord.

Blessings,
Don

Daily Praise Moment

February 22

Praising God Who Equips and Strengthens Us for Spiritual Battle (Part 2)

Ephesians 6:14-18 (NASB) says:
"14 Stand firm therefore, HAVING GIRDED YOUR LOINS WITH
TRUTH, and HAVING PUT ON THE BREASTPLATE OF
RIGHTEOUSNESS, 15 and having shod YOUR FEET WITH THE
PREPARATION OF THE GOSPEL OF PEACE; 16 in addition to all,
taking up the shield of faith with which you will be able to extinguish
all the flaming arrows of the evil ONE. 17 And take THE HELMET OF
SALVATION, and the sword of the Spirit, which is the word of God. 18
With all prayer and petition pray at all times in the Spirit, and with
this in view, be on the alert with all perseverance and petition for all
the saints. (emphasis added)

Paul was probably in prison when he wrote the church at Ephesus. At other times he was under house arrest, chained to a Roman guard. Paul had been on the spiritual battlefront ever since he became a believer, so he knew firsthand about being battle ready.

Soldiers must move quickly to engage in battle. The people of Paul's day wore long robes, and in battle a robe can present problems. Paul's advice – pull the robe between your legs, tie it securely protecting the pelvic region, and get ready for battle. Just as a swift kick in the right location can double a man over and make him defenseless, not having our loins girded with Truth can leave us defenseless. The major battleground for believers is our minds. Paul was telling the church (and us) how to be battle ready:

1. Gird your loins with Truth – give Jesus control.

2. Put on the breastplate of Righteousness – since our own righteousness is like filthy rags (Isaiah 64:6), our heart can only be protected by the Righteous One – Christ Jesus.

3. Wear shoes of Peace –let the Prince of Peace guide our steps.

4. Always carry the shield of faith – FAITH -- **F**orsaking **A**ll **I** **T**rust **H**im. As we trust Christ, Satan's flaming arrows are extinguished.

5. Wear the helmet of Salvation – Our helmet guards our minds and gives us assurance that we've been forgiven, saved, and granted eternal life. Not being sure of our salvation keeps us from being effective in our Christian walk.

6. The Sword of the Spirit – God's Word. We are to use God's Word like Jesus did when Satan tempted Him – He quoted Scripture to Satan and he left him alone.

7. Pray – be in an attitude of prayer at all times, for self and others, asking and listening as God gives us direction.

Satan hates hearing Scripture quoted to him, and he hates hearing believers praise God, so when the attacks come, quote Scripture and praise God. We must stand our ground! We can stand our ground for Satan is a defeated foe.

As I think on today's Scriptures, my musical mind begins to hear the Charles Wesley hymn, "Soldiers of Christ, Arise:"

Soldiers of Christ, arise, and put your armor on, Strong in the strength which God supplies, through His eternal Son;
Strong in the Lord of hosts, and in His mighty power,
Who in the strength of Jesus trusts, is more than conqueror.

Stand then in His great might, with all His strength endued,
And take, to arm you for the fight, the panoply (full armor) of God;
From strength to strength go on, wrestle and fight and pray;
Tread all the power of darkness down, and win the well-fought day.

Leave no unguarded place, no weakness of the soul;
Take every virtue, every grace, and fortify the whole.
That having all things done, and all your conflicts past,
Ye may over come through Christ alone, and stand complete at last.

Blessings,
Don

Daily Praise Moment

February 23

Praising Our God Who Has a Home in Heaven for Us

Psalm 48:1-3, 9-13 (NASB) says:
1 Great is the LORD, and greatly to be praised, in the city of our God,
His holy mountain. 2 Beautiful in elevation, the joy of the whole earth,
is Mount Zion in the far north, the city of the great King. 3 God, in her
palaces, has made Himself known as a stronghold.

9 We have thought on Your lovingkindness, O God, in the midst of
Your temple. 10 As is Your name, O God, so is Your praise to the ends
of the earth; Your right hand is full of righteousness. 11 Let Mount
Zion be glad, let the daughters of Judah rejoice because of Your
judgments.

12 Walk about Zion and go around her; count her towers; 13 consider
her ramparts; go through her palaces, that you may tell it to the next
generation.

Years ago as I was reading this Psalm in my daily devotions, God clearly spoke to me and said that this Psalm contained specific messages for me – truths that He wanted me to seek to apply to my daily walk with Him. The truths from this Psalm that I believe God still wants me to implement in my life are these:

God alone is worthy of our praise and adoration (v. 1).

Heaven will be an awesome place, but it is God Himself who is the stronghold (v. 3). I don't have to wait to be in Heaven to experience God's power, protection and provision – I have access to these benefits today because I've been adopted into His family.

God wants me to have a very strong relationship with Him and His kingdom (v. 12 and 13). His instruction to me to "walk about Zion, count her towers, consider her ramparts, and go through her palaces." He wants me to be more than just an acquaintance – I am to be his close, personal friend – a family member.

He wants me to be strong enough in my relationship with Him that I communicate His presence, provision and purpose to others – to tell it to the next generation (v. 13).

Seeing these truths led me that day to write this prayer in the margin of my Bible: "God, help me to know You and Your kingdom well enough to teach it to those who will follow me, my children." I'm to communicate this message to everyone who is within my circle of influence – my own family, the children I teach, friends and work associates – everyone He puts in my path.

Several years ago at a church music conference, Janet and I were blessed to have dinner with Greg Nelson, who along with his writing partner, Phill McHugh, wrote the beautiful song, "People Need the Lord." Greg told us how the song was written. He and Phill were having dinner in a restaurant and as they sat quietly and listened, they noticed that the people seated around them had very different needs. However, the greatest need that was common to each life was their need for a personal relationship with Jesus Christ. Within a matter of minutes, God inspired them to write these wonderful lyrics:

Every day, they pass me by. I can see it in their eyes.
Empty people, filled with care, headed who knows where.
On they go through private pain, living fear to fear.
Laughter hides their silent cries, only Jesus hears.

People need the Lord, people need the Lord.
At the end of broken dreams, He's the open door.
People need the Lord, people need the Lord.
When will we realize, people need the Lord.

Blessings,
Don

Daily Praise Moment

February 24

Praising Our God Who Welcomes Our Worship

John 12:1-8 says:
1 *Jesus, therefore, six days before the Passover, came to Bethany*
where Lazarus was, whom Jesus had raised from the dead. 2 *So they*
made Him a supper there, and Martha was serving; but Lazarus was
one of those reclining at the table with Him. 3 *Mary then took a pound*
of very costly perfume of pure nard, and anointed the feet of Jesus and
wiped His feet with her hair; and the house was filled with the
fragrance of the perfume. 4 *But Judas Iscariot, one of His disciples,*
who was intending to betray Him, said, 5 *"Why was this perfume not*
sold for three hundred denarii and given to poor people?" 6 *Now he*
said this, not because he was concerned about the poor, but because
he was a thief, and as he had the money box, he used to pilfer what
was put into it. 7 *Therefore Jesus said, "Let her alone, so that she may*
keep it for the day of My burial. 8 *For you always have the poor with*
you, but you do not always have Me."

After Jesus raised Lazarus from the dead, He visited Lazarus' home. Martha, Lazarus' sister, was preparing a meal when Lazarus' other sister, Mary, entered and anointed Jesus with very expensive perfume, the kind used in burial preparation. Ironically, Jesus had been teaching His disciples that His sacrificial death was imminent, but they failed to fully comprehend. However, Mary's actions seem to indicate that she understood. Judas, who was treasurer for the disciples and obviously had been stealing from the money box he carried, became angry. He criticized Mary, giving a "holier than thou" speech about how the perfume could have been sold and used to feed the poor. Jesus rebuked Judas and pointed out that the time was right for Mary's actions, saying that Judas would have plenty of time to help the poor if he truly wanted to.

Christians can come under fire when we take actions that honor Christ. Others may criticize and question our motives, but notice that the Lord honored Mary for her gift of worship. My friend, David Williams, preached on this passage at our church several years ago. Here is a quote from his sermon: "Mary came out smelling like a rose, but Judas was left holding the bag."

Jesus doesn't want us "left holding the bag." He wants our motives to be pure, and like Mary, He wants us to worship Him, recognizing that He is worthy of our worship.

As I ruminate on today's Scriptures, my musical mind begins hearing "Broken and Spilled Out" by Bill George and Gloria Gaither:

One day a plain village woman, driven by love for her Lord,
Recklessly poured out a valuable essence, disregarding the scorn.
And once it was broken and spilled out, a fragrance filled all the room.
Like a pris'ner released from his shackles, like a spirit set free from the tomb.

Broken and spilled out, just for love of You, Jesus.
My most precious treasure, lavished on Thee.
Broken and spilled out and poured at Your feet,
In sweet abandon, let me be spilled out and used up for Thee.

Lord, You were God's precious treasure, His loved and His own perfect Son. Sent here to show me the love of the Father, just for love it was done. And though You were perfect and holy, You gave up Yourself willingly. You spared no expense for my pardon, You were used up and wasted for me.

Broken and spilled out, just for love of me, Jesus.
God's most precious treasure, lavished on me.
Broken and spilled out, and poured at my feet.
In sweet abandon, Lord, You were spilled out and used up for me.

Blessings,
Don

Daily Praise Moment

February 25

Praising Our God Who Teaches and Coaches Us in How to Live for Him

Psalm 19:1, says:
The heavens declare the glory of God;
And the firmament shows His handiwork.

Psalm 19:7-11 has these words:
7 *The law of the Lord is perfect, converting the soul;*
The testimony of the Lord is sure, making wise the simple;
8 *The statutes of the Lord are right, rejoicing the heart;*
The commandment of the Lord is pure, enlightening the eyes;
9 *The fear of the Lord is clean, enduring forever;*
The judgments of the Lord are true and righteous altogether.
10 *More to be desired are they than gold,*
Yea, than much fine gold;
Sweeter also than honey and the honeycomb.
11 *Moreover by them Your servant is warned,*
And in keeping them there is great reward.

God has our best interests in His heart. He has specific plans for each of our lives. As we follow Him, we honor Him, and He uses us to make a difference in the lives of others.

As believers, God's Holy Spirit lives inside us and speaks to us with promptings to keep us on the path that God knows is best for us. For me, though, I'm convinced that I often fail to hear or respond to the promptings God gives because I'm not always open to being changed. As a result, on a daily basis God lovingly uses His "heavenly sandpaper" to sand away my rough edges to make me more like Christ.

In thinking about today's verses and how easy it is to ignore God's desire to change us, an event comes to mind from my past – a story of a young man that I worked with many years ago. This young man was well liked and got along well most of the time; however, during those times that were not in his "most of the time" category, he was a terror. He would lose his temper, throw objects and be out of control. Afterward, he would deny that he had done anything wrong.

We decided that the only way we could ever get through to him was to get video footage of one of his explosions. The camera was set up in the classroom, and soon we had a video of him "in action." When we brought him in and showed him the video of his outburst, his response was, "The videotape lies."

While this scene may cause us to chuckle now, this young man's response was much like what we say to God on a regular basis. "God, what I did wasn't really THAT bad. I do Your will MOST of the time." The reality is that when we are truly honest with God and with ourselves, we often want Our Way, instead of His Way.

My personal prayer is that I will delight in following His will. To do otherwise is to miss God's best for my life.

As I think about today's Scripture, my musical mind begins to hear this song penned by Richard D. Baker:

Walk with me blessed Lord today,
Guide my steps lest I go astray.
Thou dost know what is best for me,
I will trust and follow Thee.

Walk with me when the night is long,
Give me patience when all seems wrong;
Hear my prayer for time alone with Thee,
O Father, walk with me.

Blessings,
Don

Personal Thoughts and Prayers:

____

____

Daily Praise Moment

February 26

Praising Our God Who Equips Families to Work Together as Christ and His Church Work Together

Ephesians 5:22-32 (NASB) says:
[22] *Wives, submit to your own husbands, as to the Lord.* [23] *For the husband is head of the wife, as also Christ is head of the church; and He is the Savior of the body.* [24] *Therefore, just as the church is subject to Christ, so let the wives be to their own husbands in everything.*

[25] *Husbands, love your wives, just as Christ also loved the church and gave Himself for her,* [26] *that He might sanctify and cleanse her with the washing of water by the word,* [27] *that He might present her to Himself a glorious church, not having spot or wrinkle or any such thing, but that she should be holy and without blemish.* [28] *So husbands ought to love their own wives as their own bodies; he who loves his wife loves himself.* [29] *For no one ever hated his own flesh, but nourishes and cherishes it, just as the Lord does the church.* [30] *For we are members of His body, of His flesh and of His bones.* [31] *'For this reason a man shall leave his father and mother and be joined to his wife, and the two shall become one flesh.'* [32] *This is a great mystery, but I speak concerning Christ and the church.*

In the mid 1970s, our family was vacationing with a family that is very near and dear to us, the Overbeys. At that time, Randall & Carol and Janet and I jointly taught a Sunday evening youth class. Our children seemed more like siblings than just friends. We were all staying with Carol's precious Mom and Dad, enjoying the sunshine and waterskiing on Patrick Henry Lake in Kingsport, TN.

I awoke early on this special morning and began reading my Bible. I believe that God always speaks to us when we read the Bible if we're willing to listen, but sometimes God speaks so loudly we can't keep from hearing. I was reading Ephesians 5, thinking about the "wives, submit" and "husbands, love" verses. That morning, the light came on and I saw verse 32 *"This is a great mystery, but I speak concerning Christ and the church"* from a new perspective.

God told me that morning was that He wanted Janet and me to be as intertwined with one another as Christ is with His church. God reminded me that Christ died for His church. Also, He reminded me that the church is powerless unless it agrees with and follows Christ. It is totally a symbiotic relationship. We, as believers, are to treat one another with dignity and respect, learning from each other, honoring each other, and submitting to each other. Further, God told me that He wants Janet and me to have a home that is like a "little church" in our community, seeking to come alongside our friends and neighbors – helping them, encouraging them, and pointing them to the Savior.

As I think on today's Scripture verses, my musical mind begins to hear "We Will Be Your Church," penned by Tina English:

We have prayed and prayed concerning Your will, asking for guidance to see. And here and now, not knowing exactly how,
We want to be all we can be.

We will be Your church, Your light and Your beacon, Making Your vision our own. We will be Your church, To do what You've asked, committed to all You've begun.

We ask for strength for the job set before us, grace for the challenge ahead. Knowing the way, we can't see beyond today, but sure of the choice that we've made.

We will be Your church, Your light and Your beacon, Making Your vision our own. We will be Your church, To do what You've asked, committed to all You've begun.

We will be Your church to the lost and the needy, Reaching our arms out in love. We will be Your church, the best we can be, Completing the task, not looking back, Committed to all You've begun.

Blessings,
Don

Daily Praise Moment

February 27

Praising Our God for His Patience and Perseverance with Us

Colossians 3:12-13 (NASB) says:
[12] *So, as those who have been chosen of God, holy and beloved, put on a heart of compassion, kindness, humility, gentleness and patience;* [13] *bearing with one another, and forgiving each other, whoever has a complaint against anyone; just as the Lord forgave you, so also should you.*

And, in Romans 15:4-6 (NASB), we read:
[4] *For whatever was written in earlier times was written for our instruction, so that through perseverance and the encouragement of the Scriptures we might have hope.* [5] *Now may the God who gives perseverance and encouragement grant you to be of the same mind with one another according to Christ Jesus,* [6] *so that with one accord you may with one voice glorify the God and Father of our Lord Jesus Christ.*

Aren't you glad that God is patient with us? I certainly am. And, the way He treats us is His model for how He wants us to treat others.

As I think of people have modeled patience with me, two who come quickly to mind are Eckel Fuller and Randall Overbey. I mentioned in yesterday's Daily Praise Moment that Janet and I were privileged to vacation with Carol and Randall Overbey in her parents' home in Kingsport. Carol's mom and dad, Juanita and Eckel Fuller, were wonderful Christian folks. They modeled hospitality, love, joy, peace, patience, goodness, kindness, and all the other virtues mentioned in Galatians 5:22-23, – the "fruit of the Spirit" passage. Mr. Fuller, known as Papaw Fuggie to his grandchildren and most of the other children who often visited their home, had a ski boat that was named "Lil Scarlett." On many occasions, Mr. Fuller would say, "Let's go play on the lake."

Before I proceed with this story, though, its confession time for me. I've always enjoyed sports, but it was a rare occurrence for me to be recruited to be on a team! I was never very "sporty."

I really wanted to learn to ski, but accomplishing this task quickly was not in the equation. Randall gave me instruction on how to ski, and he and Mr. Fuller, or "Papaw Fuggie", would take me to the lake. Randall was the spotter/instructor, and Eckel was the boat driver. Some of the teenagers and adults that I taught to ski in later years would be up and skiing after two to four attempts. But me??? I'm guessing that it took, maybe 40 attempts before I succeeded.

Randall and Eckel played different roles in my skill development. Randall was my coach. He would tell me, "Keep your arms locked straight, let your knees bend up to your chest, and let the boat do the work." Eckel was my encourager. He would smile and say, "You'll get it next time." And sure enough, I finally learned to water ski. Success came when I quit trying to do it "my way." I finally listened to my instructor, followed his directions and "let the boat do the work." I even learned to ride a slalom ski the same week that I mastered two skis. But, if Randall and Eckel hadn't both been patient with me, I would have quit and felt like a failure.

The Christian life can work that way, too. As believers, God has assigned us the task of "making disciples." God wants us teaching, coaching and encouraging others to become believers and to grow in their faith. If someone is going in the wrong direction, He wants us to seek them out and bring them back.

Jeremiah 29:11, (NASB) says:
11 *For I know the plans that I have for you,' declares the LORD, 'plans for welfare and not for calamity to give you a future and a hope.*

As I think about today's Scripture verses, my musical mind begins to hear this song, penned by Richard D. Baker:

Always, yes always becoming, more like Jesus each day.
Always, yes always becoming like Jesus, my Savior and Lord.

Blessings,
Don

Daily Praise Moment

February 28

Praising Our God Who Is Trustworthy, Even in Challenging Situations

Isaiah 26:3-4 (NIV) says:
3 You will keep in perfect peace those whose minds are steadfast, because they trust in you. 4 Trust in the LORD forever, for the LORD, the LORD himself, is the Rock eternal.

No one is as trustworthy as our God. Undoubtedly, God wants all believers to learn this truth. In fact, He has been teaching us this truth all of our lives.

I'd be dishonest, though, if I said that my first response is always trust. Sometimes I do what my friends in the psychological community refer to as "reverting to my reptilian brain." Something happens that I don't expect, that I've not thought through. When this happens, I do what most people do – I hit the panic button! It is so easy for us to get into the "fight or flight" mode and think that we have to handle the situation ourselves.

The good news, though, is that God has a different plan for us. He made a way for us to work past this response. To illustrate this point, I want you to go back to Patrick Henry Lake in Kingsport with me. In earlier Daily Praise Moments, you met Eckel and Juanita Fuller and their daughter, Carol and her husband, Randall Overbey. Today, I want you to meet Carol's brother and sister-in-law, Noel and Martha Fuller. As a sidebar for all my friends who are involved in Gideons International, you may be about to see a side of serious Noel that you didn't know! Of all the people I've ever known, Noel loves playing on the lake more than anyone I've ever met. I don't remember if it was the summer that I learned to ski or the following summer, but Noel's toy that I was introduced to that summer was a rectangular kite that he pulled behind his Rayson Craft inboard ski boat. This boat had an inboard 427 cubic inch Chevy engine which generated 435 horsepower. It was very strong and fast, and it could turn on a dime. After watching Noel, Randall, and others fly the kite, I wanted to give it a try. What I didn't take to heart was the need to raise the tips of my skis as the boat lifted the kite and me off the water. Yep! You guessed it. I lost both skis during takeoff, which meant that when I finally finished the trip, I'd have to crash land – no other alternative.

An even bigger fear as we flew down the lake was getting under the two bridges that I could see. The Interstate bridge was tall, but the other bridge cleared the water by only 17 feet. As we approached the low bridge, I was looking down on cars driving across it. My first response was to panic. Options were limited. I had no skis. I could unfasten my harness and drop into the water, but I was up very high and going pretty fast. I could hold on and hope, but if Noel misjudged the boat speed as we went under the shorter bridge, I could be a bad splatter on the side of the bridge.

God said, "Trust the boat driver. He's pulled lots of people before. Your job is to hold on and enjoy the ride." When I began to trust, I saw sights I wouldn't have seen if I had remained in my panic mode.

In every situation we face, there is a space between Stimulus and Response. This space I call "God Space" or "God Time." It is the time for us to turn the matter over to God and let Him handle it. When we do, His will is accomplished. Needless to say, the trip ended well – I'm still alive, and I'll never forget the ride!!!

As I think about today's Scripture and the situation I've just described, my musical mind begins to hear "God Will Make A Way," by Don Moen:

God will make a way where there seems to be no way.
He works in ways we cannot see. He will make a way for me.
He will be my guide; hold me closely to His side.
With love and strength for each new day,
He will make a way,
He will make a way.

Blessings,
Don

Daily Praise Moment

February 29

Praising God for Using Believers to Help Other Believers

John 9:4 (NIV) says:
[4] I must work the works of Him who sent Me while it is day; the night is coming when no one can work.

Galatians 6:9 (NIV) gives us these words of encouragement:
[9] Let us not become weary in doing good, for at the proper time we will reap a harvest if we do not give up.

I have two friends whose lives have impacted each other in very positive ways – Bill Mueller and Jeff Aldridge.

Bill Mueller worked as an engineer for Alcoa Aluminum for many years. After retiring in 1991, he started volunteering with Habitat for Humanity and has helped build more than 100 Habitat homes. Last December while on a Habitat job, Bill passed out – his heart stopped beating and a medical volunteer working with him revived him. Bill was rushed to the hospital for emergency surgery where he received a pacemaker. Soon thereafter, Bill was back at work, living out his faith by helping others. Bill is now 90 years old and he is still building Habitat homes!

Bill got involved in Habitat when his church, First United Methodist Church of Maryville, Tenn. agreed to sponsor the second Habitat home built in Blount County. Bill is a member of a team of 12-15 folks who work well together, and as much as he enjoys his team, he gets the most pleasure from working alongside the prospective home owner. Bill gets great joy from "seeing the community do something good for families."

Bill's favorite Scripture is Psalm 23, and he truly knows that the Lord is his Shepherd. Bill's goal is to "wear out and not rust out"-- his dream is to be building a house when the Lord calls him home.

Jeffery Aldridge, who attends my church, has spent forty-six of his forty-eight years in a wheelchair. When he was two, a drunk driver struck Jeff's family's car and Jeffery almost lost his life. Survival seemed impossible, but Jeffrey's mother enrolled him in a treatment program which required multiple volunteers spending hours each day putting young Jeffery through patterning exercises to build muscle strength and help restore neuro pathways. Jeffery is severely disabled – he has very restricted use of both arms and legs, limited vision and handwriting ability and sometimes he has problems being understood when he speaks. However, he has a very sharp mind and is always going the extra mile to make friends. In fact, to Jeffery, a stranger is just a new friend he's never met! Jeffery calls me several times each week, or as he says, he's just giving me "a buzz" to check on me. If it is in the morning, he wants to know how I feel and if I rested well. Jeffrey prays daily for me and he always ends our conversations by wishing me a "good day and a blessed day."

Finding and maintaining employment is challenging for Jeffery, but one thing is sure – each year at Christmas he can be found outside a store on the coldest of days, heartily ringing a bell to help Salvation Army raise needed resources to minister to homeless people! When Jeffery works, he works with passion.

What ties Bill and Jeffery together is that Jeffery lives alone in a home that Bill helped build. Jeffery worked hard to develop the skills he has, and Bill worked hard to help build Jeffery's home. The strength and skill of one caring man made a way for another caring man to live independently. My challenge to you today is to find a way to use the skills and talents you have to help someone else. Remember, when we serve others, we are serving Jesus!

As I give thought to today's Scripture, my musical mind begins hearing "We'll Work till Jesus Comes," words by Elizabeth K. Mills and music by William Miller:

O land of rest, for thee I sigh! When will the moment come When I shall lay my armor by and dwell in peace at home? We'll work till Jesus comes, we'll work till Jesus comes, We'll work till Jesus comes, and we'll be gathered home.

Blessings,
Don

Public Domain

Daily Praise Moment

March 1

Praising Our God Who Is Our Friend, and Who Sends Others to Befriend Us

Luke 6:31 (NIV) records our Lord's words to His disciples spoken during the "Sermon on the Mount," where He says: *"Do to others as you would have them do to you."*

The year was 2001. I was recovering from a cerebral aneurysm. My energy level was very low. As soon as I was physically able to do so, I began going to Foothills Mall each morning with Janet. She had been going there to walk with her walking buddies for a long time. She and her friends walked six (6) half-mile laps each day in about 45-55 minutes. When I began, I could finish one lap by the time they finished all six of their laps. It was hard for me to believe that my stamina was so low and that I couldn't do any better.

A short time after I began walking, one of my friends, Bud Chandler, began walking. Bud had retired shortly before my medical problem hit. I was glad to see him. He had been my friend for almost 30 years. What I couldn't understand, though, was that Bud, who retired from active duty military service, couldn't walk any faster than I could! I had a hard time walking and talking at the same time. It took more energy than I had, but during those times when I was able to talk, Bud somehow managed to listen. And as strange as it was that Bud couldn't walk any faster than me, it was even stranger that each time I ran out of energy and had to stop for a rest, Bud was just as tired as I was and had to rest, too!

God wants us, as believers, to take the time and get involved in helping meet the needs of others. As our Lord pointed out in the Good Samaritan story, the one person who was praised was the man who took the time, got his hands dirty, spent his resources and helped. Certainly, we need to remember that we have needs, too, but if we're not careful, we can fall into the trap of "I'm just not cut out for this" or "I'm not sure I can do this," or "She was such a nice person and I want to remember her the way she was!" In each of these scenarios, the focus is on ourselves and not on the person needing help. Jesus never walked away from situations where He had to get personally involved. And, it certainly wasn't a status thing with Him, either. Remember, the same night the disciples argued over who could have the honor of sitting beside Jesus in Heaven, He washed their dirty feet.

As I think about today's Scripture and the scenario I've described, my musical mind begins to hear "Let Your Heart Be Broken," by Bryan Jeffery Leech:

Let your heart be broken for a world in need. Feed the mouths that hunger, soothe the wounds that bleed. Give a cup of water and a loaf of bread, be the hands of Jesus, serving in His stead.

Here on earth applying principles of love, visible expression God still rules above, living illustration of the Living Word To the minds of all who've never seen and heard.

Blessed to be a blessing, privileged to care, challenged by the need apparent everywhere. Where mankind is wanting fill the vacant place. Be the means thru which the Lord reveals His grace.

Add to your believing deeds that prove it true. Knowing Christ as Savior, make Him Master too: follow in His footsteps, go where He has trod, in the world's great trouble, risk yourself for God.

Let your heart be tender and your vision clear. See mankind as God sees, serve Him far and near; let your heart be broken by a brother's pain, share your rich resources, give and give again.

Blessings,
Don

Daily Praise Moment

March 2

Praising Our God for Allowing Us to See His Beauty through His Creation

Colossians 3:17 (NASB) says:
And whatever you do in word or deed, do all in the name of the Lord Jesus, giving thanks through Him to God the Father.

God equips each of us with unique gifts that He wants us to use for His glory. He wants us to minister to other believers and to reach those who are not yet believers, the lost. Remember the phrase in the Lord's Prayer, where Jesus taught His disciples to pray these words: "Thy Kingdom come, Thy will be done on earth as it is in Heaven." His will is that we use our talents and skills as He leads so His kingdom comes and His will is done here on earth, even as it is done in Heaven. In doing so, we are doing the "work of the ministry."

A small group of men from my church, Everett Hills Baptist, meets each Tuesday morning at 6:15 a.m. to pray. At the conclusion of our prayer time, we treat ourselves to a "health food" meal at Hardees. Not long ago at Hardees, I ran into my dear friend, Roger Givens, who is retired and is pursuing his passion – wildlife photography. Roger and his lovely wife, Beth, have been friends of ours for more than 45 years.

Roger has been an avid photographer all of his life. Now that he is retired, he uses much of his time to capture nature scenes. He has stunning photos of birds, butterflies, waterfalls, mountain lions, and other critters too numerous to mention. What is so unique about what Roger is doing now, though, is that he is using this "hobby" to bring honor and glory to Christ. He has published at least ten photo books. All profits made from his books go to the building fund of his church, Mt. Lebanon Baptist Church.

Roger's efforts do not stop there, though. He has compiled some of his stunning photos into multimedia presentations that he presents free of charge to churches, retirement centers, assisted living facilities, nursing homes, and civic organizations. I've seen one of his programs, "Images from The Psalms," which emphasizes God's glory through His creation. Roger has a new program that I've not yet had an opportunity to view. Beautiful background music of traditional hymns plays while the slides are being shown, and at regular points throughout the program, his slides have Bible verses intertwined, helping viewers see that Creator God is worthy of our worship. To view some of Roger's photos, visit his website: http://rogergivensphotography.com/.

As I think of today's Scripture and the way this friend is using his skills to bring glory to God, my musical mind begins to hear "This Is My Father's World," penned by Maltbie D. Babcock in 1901 and set to the music of Franklin L. Sheppard:

This is my Father's world, and to my listening ears
All nature sings, and round me rings the music of the spheres.
This is my Father's world: I rest me in the thought
Of rocks and trees, of skies and seas; His hand the wonders wrought.

This is my Father's world, the birds their carols raise,
The morning light, the lily white, declare their maker's praise.
This is my Father's world: He shines in all that's fair;
In the rustling grass I hear him pass; He speaks to me everywhere.

This is my Father's world. O let me ne'er forget
That though the wrong seems oft so strong, God is the ruler yet.
This is my Father's world: why should my heart be sad?
The Lord is King; let the heavens ring!
God reigns; let the earth be glad!

Blessings,
Don

Daily Praise Moment

March 3

Praising Our God Who Teaches Us that Serving Others Is Serving Him

Matthew 25: 44-46 (NKJV) says:
"Then they also will answer Him, saying, 'Lord, when did we see You hungry or thirsty or a stranger or naked or sick or in prison, and did not minister to You?' 45 *Then He will answer them, saying, 'Assuredly, I say to you, inasmuch as you did not do it to one of the least of these, you did not do it to Me.'* 46 *And these will go away into everlasting punishment, but the righteous into eternal life."*

I have a friend who is on Mobile Meals. As much as she enjoys the food that is brought to her, the fellowship and encouragement that she receives from the volunteers who bring her meals is what she looks forward to most. Earlier this week she was telling me about some of the conversations she had enjoyed with the people who delivered her meals.

Listening to my friend's words took me back several years to when Janet's dad was delivering Meals on Wheels. Mr. Charlie, as many people called him, always got excited about his "job." He usually started his conversations about his work by saying that he was "taking food to the old people." The reality was that he was older than most of the people he served. He had a "servant heart" and wanted to be an encourager.

Our community – really, our entire world – is in need of encouragers today. We need people who have servant hearts. Jesus' words call us to action. When we serve others, we are really serving Him.

As I think of today's Scripture, my musical mind begins to hear this Don Francisco song:

I don't care how many buses you own or the size of your sanctuary.
It doesn't matter how steep your steeple is if it's sittin' on a cemetery.
I don't care if you pave your parking lot or put pads upon your pews.
What good is picture perfect stage if you're missin' all the cues?

I don't care if your pastor's super-powered and your program's always new. What you need is love and truth and men are going to come to you. It doesn't matter that you know the Bible if it's all just in your head. The thing I need to ask you is have you done the things I said?

Do you love your wife? For her and for your children are you layin' down your life? What about the others? Are you livin' as a servant to Your sisters and your brothers? Do you make the poor man beg you for a bone? Do the widow and the orphan cry alone?

I don't care if you pray for miracles. I don't care if you speak with tongues. I don't care if you said you love Me in every song you've sung. It doesn't matter that your sacrifice of praise is loud enough to raise the dead. The thing I need to ask you is have you done the things I said?

Do you love your wife? For her and for your children are you layin' down your life? What about the others? Are you livin' as a servant to Your sisters and your brothers? Do you make the poor man beg you for a bone? Do the widow and the orphan cry alone?

Lord, when were You a prisoner that we did not come to You? When was it that we saw You sick that we didn't follow through? Every time you turned your head and pretended not to see, When you did it not to the least of these you did it not to Me.

Blessings,
Don

Daily Praise Moment

March 4

Praising Our Lord Jesus Christ Who Is The Way, The Truth and The Life

John 14:1-6 (KJV) says:
"Let not your heart be troubled; you believe in God, believe also in
Me. 2 In My Father's house are many mansions; if IT WERE not SO, I
would have told you. I go to prepare a place for you. 3 And if I go and
prepare a place for you, I will come again and receive you to Myself;
that where I am, THERE you may be also. 4 And where I go you know,
and the way you know."
5 Thomas said to Him, "Lord, we do not know where You are going,
and how can we know the way?"
6 Jesus said to him, "I am the way, the truth, and the life. No one
comes to the Father except through Me."

Life is filled with questions. But life's most important question is "What happens to me when my life is over?"

Jesus was giving His Farewell Discourse to His disciples. A sense of sadness swept over the disciples when Jesus told them that He would be betrayed and put to death. To allay their concerns, Jesus told them about Heaven and the home there that He was preparing for them and all believers. He told them that He would return for them. Then, He said that they already knew where He was going and the way to get there.

Thomas, known as the Doubter, spoke up and said what probably was on the hearts of the other disciples – "Lord, we don't know where You're going! How can we know the way?"

Jesus' response to Thomas' question gives me comfort. Jesus isn't just a way, or a truth, or a life. Jesus is The Way, The Truth and The Life. He IS the Way to Heaven. As I put my trust in Him, He takes me to His home to live with Him.

In the community where I grew up, we had a man named Garland who was well known for spinning yarns, telling tales, and misleading people with "out and out lies." Everybody loved Garland. My

Dad's favorite Garland story happened at a time when there was still an operational ferry in use, crossing the Tennessee River in downtown Loudon. One day Garland was walking briskly down the sidewalk in Loudon, and someone yelled at him and said, "Come over here and tell us a tale." Garland quickly responded, "I can't stop now, boys. A car just ran off the ferry, and I'm goin' down to see if I can help." You guessed it! Word spread up the street, and most of the folks in town that afternoon dropped what they were doing and headed down to the ferry, only to find that they had all been duped by Garland!

Take heart, my friends. Jesus never dupes us. He not only speaks the Truth, He IS The Truth. When we give Him our hearts and trust Him, He gives us eternal life.

As I think of today's Scripture, my musical mind begins to hear a high energy youth choir singing "He is the Way, He is the Truth, He is the Life," written by Otis Skillings and arranged by Mosie Lister:

God sent His Son to be our Savior. (repeat 3 times)
He is the Way; He is the Truth; He is the Life.

'Twas Jesus Christ who came to save the world (repeat 3 times) He
is the Way; He is the Truth; He is the Life.

He gave His life that we might be set free; (repeat 3 times)
He is the Way; He is the Truth; He is the Life.

Rose from the grave that we might live again; (repeat 3 times)
He is the Way; He is the Truth; He is the Life.

He lives today; I know He always will. (repeat 3 times)
He is the Way; He is the Truth; He is the Life.

God sent His Son to be our Savior; (repeat 3 times)
He is the Way; He is the Truth; He is the Life.

Blessings,
Don

Daily Praise Moment

March 5

Praising Our God Who Paid Our Sin Debt and Offers to Adopt Us into His Family

Romans 5:8-10 (NKJV) says:
8 *But God demonstrates His own love toward us, in that while we were*
still sinners, Christ died for us. 9 *Much more then, having now been*
justified by His blood, we shall be saved from wrath through Him.
10 *For if when we were enemies we were reconciled to God through the*
death of His Son, much more, having been reconciled, we shall be
saved by His life.

These verses contain many wonderful Bible truths.

First, God took the initiative for our salvation. We don't have to clean ourselves up and then come to Him. As verse 8 says, *While we were still sinners, Christ died for us!*

Second, because Christ died for us, the penalty of our sin has been paid. We've been "justified."

The Holman Bible Dictionary defines justification as the "process by which an individual is brought into an unmerited, right relationship with a person, whether that relationship is established between people or with God." I heard a preacher explain justification in this way – He said, "When I was 'justified,' my spiritual relationship with God was 'Just (as) if I'd' never sinned."

Finally, we've been reconciled. The Holman Bible Dictionary defines reconciliation as "The establishment of friendly relations between parties who are at variance with each other, making peace after an engagement in war, or readmission to the presence and favor of a person after rebellion against the person."

Another word for "reconciliation" is Atonement. As believers, we have Atonement, or "At-One-Ment" with God through our Lord Jesus Christ. Once we surrender to His Lordship, we're members of His family.

I heard a story about an event which happened during the Civil War era. According to the story, there was a group of outlaws in the Southwest who called themselves the Quantrill Raiders. This group brought havoc on people, robbing them, burning their property, then riding off to safety. Finally, many of them were caught and were about to be executed, when out of the blue, a young man ran up in front of the firing squad and yelled, "Wait." He pointed to one of the men who was about to be executed and explained that this man had a wife and four children who needed him. Then, he said, "I'm guilty. Let me die in his place." After discussing the matter, the officers in charge granted the request. Later, the man whose life had been spared retrieved the body of the man who died in his place and gave him a proper burial. The inscription that he put on the man's tombstone was, "He took my place. He died for me."

Christ took our place – He died for us.

As I think of today's Scriptures, my musical mind begins to hear "When I Survey the Wondrous Cross," penned by Isaac Watts in 1707:

When I survey the wondrous cross on which the Prince of glory died, my richest gain I count but loss, and pour contempt on all my pride.

Forbid it, Lord, that I should boast, save in the death of Christ my God! All the vain things that charm me most, I sacrifice them to His blood.

See from His head, His hands, His feet, sorrow and love flow mingled down! Did e'er such love and sorrow meet, or thorns compose so rich a crown?

Were the whole realm of nature mine, that were a present far too small; Love so amazing, so divine, demands my soul, my life, my all.

Blessings,
Don

Daily Praise Moment

March 6

Praising The Lord Jesus Christ -- The Ultimate Example of Right Living

Proverbs 6:20-22 New American Standard Bible (NASB), says: *"20 My son, observe the commandment of your father And do not forsake the teaching of your mother. 21 Bind them continually on your heart; Tie them around your neck. 22 When you walk about, they will guide you; When you sleep, they will watch over you; And when you awake, they will talk to you."*

God wants all children to internalize godly values and morals so they can live peaceable, godly lives. When we stop and observe, the reality is that they are learning values from us, whether we like it or not. That is why it is so important to strive to be an example of godly living.

When my son, Vance, was a small child, he and I went arrowhead hunting occasionally with my dad. Daddy got around well, but he had a very bad limp that was the result of a gunshot wound that he miraculously survived. Dad's pace was a bit slower than others. Without a functional hip or knee joint on the left side, he would swing his left leg as he walked. His left leg was also about an inch shorter than his right leg, so when he walked, instead of his head staying level, it would go up or down, depending on which foot was making contact with the ground. The soil of the field we were in was freshly plowed red clay dirt, and it was on a hillside.

As Daddy walked, Vance followed his every step. I was intrigued that my young son was stepping in each footprint that his Papaw made. However, as I watched more closely, I noticed something more intriguing. My young son was walking with the exact same stride that my daddy was walking, and my son didn't realize he was doing it!

All of us are modeling for others. God wants us to model His behavior so that the next generation learns to walk the way Christ walked.

As I think of today's Scripture and the way God wants us to be positive role models for the next generation, my musical mind begins to hear "Let Others See Jesus in You," penned by B. B. McKinney in 1924:

While passing thro' this world of sin,
and others your life shall view,
Be clean and pure without, within;
Let others see Jesus in you.

Let others see Jesus in you,
Let others see Jesus in you.
Keep telling the story, be faithful and true;
Let others see Jesus in you.

Your life's a book before their eyes,
They're reading it thro' and thro'
Say, does it point them to the skies,
Do others see Jesus in you?

Let others see Jesus in you,
Let others see Jesus in you.
Keep telling the story, be faithful and true;
Let others see Jesus in you.

Then live for Christ both day and night,
Be faithful, be brave and true,
and lead the lost to life and light.
Let others see Jesus in you.

Let others see Jesus in you,
Let others see Jesus in you.
Keep telling the story, be faithful and true,
Let others see Jesus in you.

Blessings,
Don

PS Thank you for being that godly example for others to follow.

Daily Praise Moment

March 7

Praising Our God Who Shepherds Us to Grow in Our Faith

Colossians 1:9-12 (NKJV) says:
*"[11] For this reason we also, since the day we heard it, do not cease to
pray for you, and to ask that you may be filled with the knowledge of
His will in all wisdom and spiritual understanding; [10] that you may
walk worthy of the Lord, fully pleasing Him, being fruitful in every
good work and increasing in the knowledge of God; [11] strengthened
with all might, according to His glorious power, for all patience and
longsuffering with joy; [12] giving thanks to the Father who has qualified
us to be partakers of the inheritance of the saints in the light."*

We have a woman in our church, Shirley, who is the consummate volunteer. Almost any time you see her, she is providing transportation to someone, lending a helping hand, playing piano and providing birthday gifts for everyone in the assisted living facility that our church visits each week. If you say something to Shirley to acknowledge her for what she is doing, she'll respond by saying, "Don't thank me. I haven't done anything." Then, she smiles with a contagious smile and walks away.

I've admired this facet of Shirley's life for a long time. She made me rethink my own behavior a few months ago, though, when I made a comment on how clean her car was.

To me, a car is a tool to get from Point A to Point B. Prior to Shirley's comment, my description of cleaning a car was to take it to a carwash, put in my quarters, spray on the soap, rinse it and drive off. After I commented on Shirley's car looking so beautiful, I said, "Where do you go to wash your car?"

Shirley's response was, "The only time I go to a carwash is when I'm in a hurry. A carwash gets some dirt off, but I usually have to go home and wash it again."

I thought about what she said and suddenly felt convicted. I went to the Autozone, bought car wash and an appropriate cloth, came home and washed my car. To my surprise, the car looked much better than I'd ever thought it could look. Now, don't get me wrong. Compared to Shirley's car, my car usually looks much dirtier, but I'm taking action now that I never took before. I see things differently.

This experience made me question how I was living my life with God, too. Was I cutting corners in my daily walk? Was I giving God the time and attention I needed to give Him to fully experience the relationship that He wanted to have with me?

God wants a dynamic relationship with each of His children; a relationship of trust, growth, and ongoing communication.

As I think of today's Scripture, my musical mind begins to hear "The Greatest Thing," written by Mark Pendergrass:

The greatest thing in all my life is knowing You.
The greatest thing in all my life is knowing You.
I want to know You more. I want to know You more.
The Greatest thing in all my life is knowing You.

The greatest thing in all my life is loving You.
The greatest thing in all my life is loving You.
I want to love You more. I want to love You more.
The Greatest thing in all my life is loving You.

The greatest thing in all my life is serving You.
The greatest thing in all my life is serving You.
I want to serve You more. I want to serve You more.
The Greatest thing in all my life is serving You.

Blessings,
Don

Daily Praise Moment

March 8

Praising Our God Who Is Far Greater Than We Can Ever Imagine

Ephesians 3:20-21 (NKJV) says:
"Now to Him who is able to do exceedingly abundantly above all that we ask or think, according to the power that works in us, [21] to Him be glory in the church by Christ Jesus to all generations, forever and ever. Amen."

In the spring of 1992, Daniel and I began taking scuba diving lessons. We completed the classes and went with our dive group to Florida to do our "check-out" dives for certification.

The first dive was at Madison Blue Springs. Madison Blue is now a State Park, but at the time of our dive, it was unregulated. Madison Blue is a first magnitude, crystal clear spring. The cave entrance from which the spring projects water is about 25 feet deep, and the limestone pool is 82 feet wide. The volume of water that this spring is releasing is HUGE. Everyone in our group immediately began having a wonderful time.

To get to the mouth of the spring, we would swim above it and let some of the air out of our buoyancy compensator (BC) vests. As we did this, we slowly sank into the path of the water projecting from the cave. The force of the water made you feel like you were being shot from a cannon. I watched with delight as Daniel would float over the cave entrance, then be shot out of it about 15 to 20 feet. He would quickly swim back, roll over on his back, fold his arms, cross his legs and smile like he was enjoying the "Life of Riley."

We made several dives on this trip in multiple locations. Some of the sink holes into which we dove were covered with algae and looked horrible on the surface, but once we were underneath, we were seeing a brand new world that I'd never even imagined existed.

A year later, Dan and I went to Ginnie Springs and did diving. After diving to the mouth of Devil's Eye Cave, we floated down the Suwannee River to go into another spring. The water in the river was coffee colored due to tannic acid from decaying leaves. We didn't know it until we were in a location where crystal clear spring water was discharging into the river that swimming beside us were several gar fish that were almost as big as we were!

Like the thrill of seeing underwater sights never imagined, God leads us to experience aspects of His person, power and glory as we go through life. Like the algae pools, the tannic acid water and the big gar fish, sometimes these opportunities to get to know God better, look very scary. We face hard times – times when it seems we are alone. But as we trust Him and lean on His sufficiency, we start to understand that His power and greatness are far more than we could ever think or imagine.

As I read today's Scripture and think on the events that I've just described, my musical mind begins to hear "I Can Only Imagine," an enchanting song, by MercyMe:

I can only imagine what it will be like when I walk by your side.
I can only imagine what my eyes will see when your face is before me.
I can only imagine, I can only imagine.

Surrounded by Your glory, what will my heart feel?
Will I dance for you Jesus or in awe of you be still?
Will I stand in your presence or to my knees will I fall?
Will I sing hallelujah, will I be able to speak at all?
I can only imagine, I can only imagine.

Blessings,
Don

Daily Praise Moment

March 9

Praising Our God, the Faithful One Who Always Keeps His Promises

2 Corinthians 1:20 (NKJV) says:
20 For all the promises of God in Him ARE Yes, and in Him Amen, to the glory of God through us.

1 Thessalonians 5:24 (NKJV), has these words:
24 He who calls you IS faithful, who also will do IT.

When Daniel was 13, he and some of his friends were riding bikes in our backyard. I went out to visit with them. I was "trying to reconnect" with my teenage son. Vance was a UT student, living in Knoxville. I was working full-time at Tennessee School for the Deaf, serving as part-time music director at our church and trying to complete a doctorate, all at the same time. It saddens me to say that I was operating under the myth that there was such a thing as "quality time" that made up for all the time I was missing.

At just the right moment, Dan said, "Dad, do you remember that tree house that you PROMISED me, but never got around to building?"

I said, "Yes, Daniel, I remember, and I'm sorry."

Dan said, "Dad, it's okay. I don't want a tree house any more. What I REALLY want now is a skateboard half-pipe!"

I don't know if it was my guilt over promising something that I never delivered, guilt over not spending time with my kids, or listening to God saying to me that this was an opportunity to build a better relationship with my son; but before I really stopped to think about it, I said, "Okay."

I'm a lousy builder – but Dan and I went to Home Depot with my trailer and bought supplies. We began working together. In order to avoid a major catastrophe, we decided that the ramp had to be 12 feet wide.

After the two of us invested time and lots of energy, Daniel had a ramp that was almost six feet high on each end and twelve feet wide and 50 feet long. As we were finishing the ramp, worry kicked in. In my mind, I was saying, "What have I done?" I wrote up a Parent Permission Form that had to be signed and had a rule that skating could only occur when adult supervision was present. My rules were followed -- maybe a week! Miraculously, in the time Daniel had the ramp, no bones were broken. Looking back, I'm glad that Dan and I were able to build the ramp. Having it in our yard let me know where my son and his friends were most days. And Janet and I had the joy of getting to know Daniel and his friends much better.

Unlike my broken promise to Daniel, God's promises are always kept. Unlike me who was gone a lot of the time, our Omnipresent God is always with us. Unlike me being too weak and inadequate to meet the challenge of staying connected, our Omnipotent God is more than able to meet each challenge. Unlike me, God is Omniscient. He knows my needs, even before I ask.

As I think of today's Scripture, my musical mind begins to hear this song, written by Janet Paschal:

It must have felt strange to end up stranded, between an army and the sea. They must have felt forsaken, wondering why God wasn't all He said He'd be. When your back's against the wall, that's the hardest place of all, but somewhere between provision and impossibility: God will make a way where there seems to be no way, forever He is faithful. He will make a road when you bear a heavy load. I know, God will make a way.

When a wall of circumstances leaves you cryin' in the night, And you struggle till your strength is almost gone, God will gently hold you in the shelter of His heart, He'll carve a road for you to carry on. So carry on, Travel on! God will make a way where there seems to be no way, forever He is faithful. He will make a road when you have a heavy load. I know, that God will make a way.

Blessings,
Don

Daily Praise Moment

March 10

Praising Our God Who Transforms Us into His Likeness as We Focus on Him

2 Corinthians 3:18 (NKJV) says:
But we all, with unveiled face, beholding as in a mirror the glory of the Lord, are being transformed into the same image from glory to glory, just as by the Spirit of the Lord.

I remember a country song that had words something like these:

I was a lookin' back to see if you was lookin' back to see
If I was lookin' back to see if you was lookin' back at me.
You was cute as you could be, standin' lookin' back at me
And it was plain to see, that I'd enjoy your company.

Do you remember going into the "House of Mirrors" at the county fair when you were a kid? I do. Each mirror gave a different impression of what I looked like. In some of the mirrors, my head was HUGE. In others, my upper body would be thin, but my feet and legs would be gigantic or as my granddaughters used to say, "ginormous."

When I went to college and began studying sociology, one of the authors I read was Charles Horton Cooley. In 1902, Cooley wrote that a person's self-image grows out of one's interactions with others. As a person observes the feedback he gets from others, the person forms a mental image of himself. Cooley called this the "Looking Glass Self." Cooley summarized his theory with these words: "I am not what I think I am, and I am not what you think I am; I am what I think that you think I am."

I don't remember the source of this comment, but somewhere along my life's way I was told that the way our government trains people to detect counterfeit money is to have the person study legitimate currency and observe the details.

God is making each of us in a unique way, fashioning us by His hands to do His work. He molds and shapes us to be the special people He wants us to be, uniquely equipped for our greater good and His greater glory. As we look intently at Him, He shapes us to look more and more like Him.

As I reflect on today's Scripture, my musical mind begins to hear two songs, "When I Look Into Your Holiness" by Wayne and Cathy Perrin, and "Turn Your Eyes Upon Jesus, by Helen Lemmel:

When I look into Your holiness, when I gaze into Your loveliness
When all the things that surround become shadows in the light of You,
I worship You, I worship You. The reason I live is to worship You.

O soul, are you weary and troubled? No light in the darkness you see?
There's light for a look at the Savior, and life more abundant and free!

Turn your eyes upon Jesus, look full in His wonderful face,
And the things of earth will grow strangely dim, in the light of His glory and grace.

Through death into life everlasting, He passed, and we follow Him there; O'er us sin no more hath dominion — For more than con-q'rors we are!

His Word shall not fail you — He promised; Believe Him, and all will be well: Then go to a world that is dying, His perfect salvation to tell!

Turn your eyes upon Jesus, look full in His wonderful face,
And the things of earth will grow strangely dim,
In the light of His glory and grace.

Blessings,
Don

Daily Praise Moment

March 11

Praising Our God Who Guides Us, Provides for Us and Protects Us

Psalm 23 (NKJV) says:
The Lord is my shepherd; I shall not want. 2 He makes me to lie down in green pastures; He leads me beside the still waters. 3 He restores my soul; He leads me in the paths of righteousness For His name's sake. 4 Yea, though I walk through the valley of the shadow of death, I will fear no evil; For You are with me; Your rod and Your staff, they comfort me. 5 You prepare a table before me in the presence of my enemies; You anoint my head with oil; My cup runs over. 6 Surely goodness and mercy shall follow me All the days of my life; And I will dwell in the house of the Lord forever.

Few passages in the Bible are better known than Psalm 23. When I go through tough times in my life, I often go to sleep repeating this wonderful Psalm.

Psalm 23:1 takes on different meanings based on which word in the first sentence is emphasized. If I say, "The LORD is my shepherd," my focus is on the omnipotence of our LORD. If I say, "The Lord IS my shepherd," my emphasis is on the omnipresence of the Lord, of His being in the here and now with me. If I say, "The Lord is MY shepherd," I'm emphasizing the personal relationship that I have with Christ. If I say, "The Lord is my SHEPHERD," I'm emphasizing the protection and care of our Savior. God wants us to learn all these meanings and to grow in our faith toward our Savior.

Verse 4 talks about walking through the "valley of the shadow of death." Shadows, like some of God's creatures, may appear scary. In reality, shadows have no power over us unless we give power to them. God wants us to use our minds and make discerning decisions, but He also wants us to trust Him and not just succumb to fear.

God IS our SHEPHERD. He protects us. He keeps us. He provides for us. Shadows are just shadows, and shadows dissipate when we travel in the LIGHT.

As I think about today's Scripture, my musical mind begins to hear soloist Sheron McGill and our church choir singing, "I Know," penned by Laverne Tripp, Ervin Rouse, Morry Burns and Lois Mann:

Some people say this old-time religion is just a thing of the past.
But in this modern age that we're living, it's the only thing that will last. Now you may think I'm a little old fashioned. Well, friend, that's alright with me. I'm so glad that I am a Christian and from sin I have been set free.

I know, I know, there's no doubt about it, He lives in my heart, and I'm gonna shout it. I know, I know, my sins are forgiven, and I'm on my way to a place that's called heaven.

Not long ago, at an old fashioned altar, I knelt on my knees there in prayer. He lifted my burdens; sin's shackles fell from me, and His presence was so real everywhere. Now that the load I carried is lighter, it changed my grey skies to blue. My steps are now higher for I have this assurance that His sweet love will carry me through.

Come, go with me to the land over yonder He's prepared for the pure and the true. It's a place where sickness and death cannot enter. I'm going, brother, how about you? Maybe today or maybe tomorrow, He'll return in robes of pure white. I'm packing up now getting my things together. Who Knows? He may come tonight.

I know, I know, there's no doubt about it, He lives in my heart, and I'm gonna shout it. I know, I know, my sins are forgiven, And I'm on my way to a place that's called heaven.

Blessings,
Don

Daily Praise Moment

March 12

Praising Our God Who Has a Heavenly Home Prepared for His Children

John 14:1-3 (NKJV) records Jesus' words to His disciples before His crucifiction:
"Let not your heart be troubled; you believe in God, believe also in Me. [2] In My Father's house are many mansions; if it were not so, I would have told you. I go to prepare a place for you. [3] And if I go and prepare a place for you, I will come again and receive you to Myself; that where I am, there you may be also."

Psalm 139:16 (NKJV) says:
"Your eyes saw my substance, being yet unformed. And in Your book they all were written, the days fashioned for me, when as yet there were none of them."

I've been acquainted with death and dying my entire life, but when my younger brother, Larry died at the age of 43, it really hit me hard. I was particularly sad because I have the same inherited illness that Larry had. I spent about two months in the doldrums, feeling sad about Larry's suffering and the fact that he had died so young. Larry had aged rapidly as his disease progressed. One event that bothered me was when a respiratory therapist told me to bring MY DAD over closer to the equipment so he could hook him up for a treatment. He was talking about Larry, my younger brother!

I knew the truth of John 14:1-6, where Jesus taught about our heavenly home. I knew that Jesus said that He was the Way, the Truth and the Life and we experience eternal life by trusting in Him. I knew that Larry had a personal relationship with Christ and he was in heaven. And I knew that Psalm 139:16 tells us that before we breathed our first breath, our days were written down in God's book. Yet, I was still focusing on Larry's suffering and our loss.

In early January after Larry's death, Janet and I attended a music conference. Kim Noblitt , a member of the musical group, TRUTH, gave a testimony before singing a song he had written. Kim shared that one of his friends had died and he had been asked by his friend's wife to sing at the memorial service. He was ready to go, but a snowstorm hit; flights were cancelled, and he couldn't make the trip. That night, as he grieved his friend's passing and experienced the frustration of not being able to go to his friend's memorial, God gave him a song. As I sat and listened to his story, tears streamed down my cheeks. The tears stopped though, as I listened to "If You Could See Me Now," the song God had inspired Kim to write:

Our prayers have all been answered. I finally arrived.
The healing that had been delayed has now been realized.
No one's in a hurry. There's no schedule to keep.
We're all enjoying Jesus, just sitting at His feet.

Chorus:
If you could see me now, I'm walking streets of gold.
If you could see me now, I'm standing strong and whole.
If you could see me now, you'd know I've seen His face.
If you could see me now, you'd know the pain is erased.
You wouldn't want me to ever leave this place,
If you could only see me now.

My light and temporary trials have worked out for my good,
To know it brought Him glory when I misunderstood.
Oh yes, we've had our sorrows, but they can never compare.
What Jesus has in store for us, no language can share.

(Chorus twice)

You wouldn't want me to ever leave this perfect place
If you could only see me now
If you could see me now
If you could only see me now

Blessings,
Don

Daily Praise Moment

March 13

Praising Our God Who Affords Us the Opportunity to Serve Him

Titus 1:1-4 (The Message), says:
I, Paul, am God's slave and Christ's agent for promoting the faith among God's chosen people, getting out the accurate word on God and how to respond rightly to it. My aim is to raise hopes by pointing the way to life without end. This is the life God promised long ago — and he doesn't break promises! And then when the time was ripe, he went public with his truth. I've been entrusted to proclaim this Message by order of our Savior, God himself. Dear Titus, legitimate son in the faith: Receive everything God our Father and Jesus our Savior give you!

Paul identified himself as a bondservant or slave of God. His task was to "promote the faith among God's chosen people, teaching them to rightly respond."

Like Paul, the challenge that God has given us today is to see ourselves as His bondservants, too.

Remember what Jesus said in Matthew 22:37-40 (NKJV), after He was asked which commandment was the greatest?
37 Jesus said to him, "'You shall love the Lord your God with all your heart, with all your soul, and with all your mind.' 38 This is the first and great commandment. 39 And the second is like it: 'You shall love your neighbor as yourself.' 40 On these two commandments hang all the Law and the Prophets."

Think about it – We, as believers, are entrusted with the opportunity and responsibility to "change the world," one person at a time. We do so by loving individuals into His Kingdom.

In our God-assigned role, a summary of our resume looks like this:
Job Title – Christian (Bondservant)
Employer – God
Supervisor – The Holy Spirit
Trainer/Example – The Lord Jesus Christ
Place of Employment – Home, Work, School, Church, Community

Remember His call to us in Matthew 28:19 – *"As you are going, make disciples!"*

As I reflect on today's Scripture verses, my musical mind begins to hear "They'll Know We Are Christians by Our Love," written by Peter Scholtes:

We are one in the Spirit, we are one in the Lord
We are one in the Spirit, we are one in the Lord
And we pray that all unity may one day be restored

And they'll know we are Christians by our love, by our love
Yes, they'll know we are Christians by our love

We will work with each other, we will work side by side
We will work with each other, we will work side by side
And we'll guard each one's dignity and save each one's pride

And they'll know we are Christians by our love, by our love
Yes, they'll know we are Christians by our love

We will walk with each other, we will walk hand in hand
We will walk with each other, we will walk hand in hand
And together we'll spread the news that God is in our land

And they'll know we are Christians by our love, by our love
Yes, they'll will know we are Christians by our love

Blessings,
Don

Daily Praise Moment

March 14

Praising Our God Who Equips Us with His Word So We Can Be Victorious

1 Peter 5:8-9 (NKJV) says:
8 Be sober, be vigilant; because your adversary the devil walks about
like a roaring lion, seeking whom he may devour. 9 Resist him,
steadfast in the faith, knowing that the same sufferings are experienced
by your brotherhood in the world.

Hebrews 4:12 (NKJV) says,
12 For the word of God is living and powerful, and sharper than any two-edged sword, piercing even to the division of soul and spirit, and of joints and marrow, and is a discerner of the thoughts and intents of the heart.

When I was a child, I had an elderly neighbor whose name was Miss Nettie. Miss Nettie was about 4.5 feet tall, always wore a bonnet a long apron, and shoes like Granny Clampett. She lived alone, grew a garden, raised cows and chickens, and sold eggs. She didn't drive. She was a close friend of my neighbor and Sunday school teacher, Mrs. Ina Mae Shaw. When our junior boys Sunday school class had a picnic, Miss Nettie would come along. If we hiked in the woods, Miss Nettie would bend a small sapling over and show us young boys how to "ride a horse." She was full of life.

When Miss Nettie was young, she broke her arm, and the arm was never set. One of her favorite activities was to ask us boys, "Which one of you can kiss his own elbow?" We would all try and fail, but not Miss Nettie. She would twist her arm that had not been set, and plant a kiss on her own elbow! We lived out in the country, and everyone had a dog. Dogs would bark and growl to keep people off their family's property. Some would come out into the road and chase you, but they all gave Miss Nettie plenty of space because, in addition to the large basket that she carried with the eggs and Watkins products she sold, she carried a tool for self-preservation. She always carried a bug spray pump. If a dog threatened, she would spray it in the dog's direction and the dog would quickly retreat.

As believers, God wants us to be armed with a tool of self-preservation, too. Not only is God's Word a "lamp unto our feet" and a "light unto our path," it is a tool that we can use to silence the enemy. Remember when Satan tempted our Lord? Jesus answered Satan by quoting Scripture verses to him.

Ephesians 6:17 (NKJV) says:
[17] And take the helmet of salvation, and the sword of the Spirit, which is the word of God;

Romans 8:31-32 (NKJV) says:
[31] What then shall we say to these things? If God is for us, who can be against us?[32] He who did not spare His own Son, but delivered Him up for us all, how shall He not with Him also freely give us all things?

As I think on today's Scripture, my musical mind begins to hear "The Battle Belongs to the Lord," by Jamie Owens-Collins:

In heavenly armor we'll enter the land. The battle belongs to the Lord.
No weapon that's fashioned against us shall stand.
The battle belongs to the Lord.

We sing glory and honor, power and strength to the Lord.
We sing glory and honor, power and strength to the Lord.

The power of darkness comes in like a flood. The battle belongs to the Lord. He's raised up a standard, the power of His blood. The battle belongs to the Lord.

When your enemy presses in hard, do not fear. The battle belongs to the Lord. Take courage my friend, your redemption is near. The battle belongs to the Lord.

We sing glory and honor, power and strength to the Lord.
We sing glory and honor, power and strength to the Lord.

Blessings,
Don

Daily Praise Moment

March 15

Praising Our God Who Forgives Our Trespasses As We Forgive Others

Ephesians 4:32 (NIV) says,
Be kind and compassionate to one another, forgiving each other, just as in Christ, God forgave you.

In Matthew 6:12, where Jesus was teaching His disciples how to pray, He told them to pray and ask God to *"forgive us our debts* (our trespasses and sins) *AS WE ALSO HAVE FORGIVEN OUR DEBTORS."*

I'd prayed The Lord's Prayer over and over for years without realizing what I was asking God to do. Then, it "hit me." I saw how serious the Lord's Prayer really is. As I pray this prayer, I'm asking God to forgive me with the same measure as I forgive others. So, if I'm unwilling to forgive others when they hurt me, I'm praying and asking God to NOT forgive me!!! That's hard.

Forgiving others not only is a key to being forgiven, it is a key to personal freedom.

A few years ago, a close friend of mine was going through a very hard time. He was at a point where he felt that life was caving in on him – he was talking about ending his own life. He didn't want to live anymore with the hurt that he was carrying.

When we met to talk and pray, we prayed a simple prayer together that went something like this:

"Heavenly Father, we come to you in Jesus' name and ask you to bring to my friend's mind all those who have hurt him that he has never forgiven. He wants to be free from the bondage of having an unforgiving heart."

Immediately after praying this prayer, names and situations began to flood his mind. Some of the people and incidents were from childhood, where people taunted him and called him names.

We made a list of the names and hurts that had been done to him. Within about 30 minutes, he had a list of 35 names. Just getting the names and situations on paper gave a bit of relief.

Then, he prayed a prayer similar to this:
"Lord Jesus, Your Word in Matthew 6:12 tells me to pray, asking You to forgive my trespasses just as I forgive others for their trespasses against me. As an act of my will, I choose to forgive __________ (name the person) for ________________ (name the activity or wrong action done). Romans 12:19 (NIV), says, "Do not take revenge, my dear friends, but leave room for God's wrath, for it is written: "It is mine to avenge; I will repay, says the Lord." "I choose to let this person off my hook. This problem is no longer mine. I'm giving it to You to handle. I reclaim the ground in my mind where this memory / hurt has been living, and I give this part of my mind over to Your control. Have Your will and way in my life. Thank You for freeing me of this past hurt."

As my friend prayed through his list of 35 names, a lot of the tension that had been holding him captive left, and he began to heal.

When we hold onto anger, hatred and disgust, we are letting Satan control a portion of our minds. I believe that he uses this as a staging area to attack us. His attacks can take at least two forms:

1. He will use past hurts to prevent us from having meaningful relationships with others. We can carry distrust with us to the point that we are always second-guessing the motives of others.

2. He can accuse us and say to us, "You must not be a real Christian. A real Christian wouldn't be holding onto the anger you're holding on to." Satan does this to try to prevent us from experiencing freedom in Christ. He knows that if we are in bondage, we won't be effective witnesses.

Remember what John 10:10 says: "The thief (Satan) comes only to steal, kill and destroy, but I come that they might have life, and have it abundantly." The Lord wants us to have freedom from past hurts.

As I mull over today's Scriptures, my musical mind begins to hear "Be Ye Glad," by Michael Kelly Blanchard:

In these days of confused situations,
In this night of a restless remorse
When the heart and the soul of a nation
Lay wounded and cold as a corpse,
From the grave of the innocent Adam
Comes a song bringing joy to the sad.
Oh, your cry has been heard
And the ransom
Has been paid up in full, be ye glad.

Oh, be ye glad, Oh, be ye glad.
Every debt that you've ever had
Has been paid up in full by the grace of the Lord.
Be ye glad, be ye glad, be ye glad.

So be like lights on the rim of the water
Giving hope in a storm sea of night.
Be a refuge amidst the slaughter
Of these fugitives in their flight
For you are timeless and part of a puzzle
You are winsome and young as a lad
And there is no disease or no struggle
That can pull you from God, be ye glad.

Oh, be ye glad, Oh, be ye glad.
Every debt that you ever had
Has been paid up in full by the grace of the Lord.
Be ye glad, be ye glad, be ye glad.

Oh, be ye glad, Oh, be ye glad

Every debt that you ever had
Has been paid up in full by the grace of the Lord.
Be ye glad, be ye glad, be ye glad.

Blessings,
Don

Heavenly Father,
Please bring to my mind the people who have hurt me that I've never forgiven. By faith, I choose to forgive the following people for the following hurts:

PERSON	HURT

Thank You, Lord, for giving me the strength to forgive. Thank You, too, Lord, for the freedom that comes as I forgive.

I reclaim the part of my life that previously was under Satan's control and ask You to use me to help others be free.

I pray this prayer in the name that is above every name, the Lord Jesus Christ, Your Son and my Savior.
Amen

Daily Praise Moment

March 16

Praising God Makes a Way for Us, Even When We Face Overwhelming Dangers

Exodus 15:1-2 (NIV) says,
Then Moses and the Israelites sang this song to the LORD:
"I will sing to the LORD, for He is highly exalted.
Both horse and driver He has hurled into the sea."
2 *"The LORD is my strength and my defense;*
He has become my salvation."

Under God's direction, Moses led the Israelite nation out of bondage in Egypt. Remember the scene at the Red Sea? Moses and all of the people went to the seashore. The Egyptian army was chasing them, quickly gaining ground. The people of Israel were caught "between a rock and a hard place." There was nowhere to turn. If they stood still, Pharaoh's army would kill them. If they marched into the Red Sea, they would all surely drown.

The children of Israel began to cry out to the Lord, but their cries were not cries of faith. They were cries of fear. They immediately began blaming Moses, saying that he had brought them out into the wilderness to die.

Have you ever felt trapped? Bad circumstances in front of you and equally bad problems pressing down on you from behind?

Fortunately, Moses saw God instead of just the problem. He told the children of Israel (Exodus 14:13) to "Fear not, stand still and see the salvation of the Lord."

The Lord spoke to Moses and said (Exodus 14:15), "Why is everyone crying out to me? You, Moses, speak to the children of Israel and tell them to go forward." Then God told Moses to lift the rod of Aaron over the sea and divide the water. When Moses did so, the waters parted, and the children of Israel walked through on dry land. God put the Pillar of Cloud that led the children of Israel during the day between the Israelites and the Egyptians so the Egyptians had to slow down their pursuit.

When the children of children Israel were safe on the other side, the Egyptian army marched into sea bed between the pillars of water. God told Moses to stretch out his hand again over the waters. Moses obeyed and the waters returned, drowning the Egyptian army.

We all face battles in our lives. Our choice is the same as Moses faced. We must ask ourselves, "Do I focus on the problem, or do I focus on the Lord Jesus Christ, my Savior?"

As I think of today's Scripture, my musical mind begins to hear "Let My People Go," and "Thank You, Lord," by Bessie and Seth Sykes:

When Israel was in Egypt's land, "Let My people go!"
Oppressed so hard they could not stand, "Let My people go!"

Refrain:
"Go down, Moses, way down in Egypt's land;
Tell old Pharaoh to let My people go!"

No more shall they in bondage toil, "Let My people go!"
Let them come out with Egypt's spoil, "Let My people go!"

Oh, let us all from bondage flee, "Let My people go!"
And let us all in Christ be free, "Let My people go!"

You need not always weep and mourn, "Let My people go!"
And wear these slav'ry chains forlorn, "Let My people go!"

Your foes shall not before you stand, "Let My people go!"
And you'll possess fair Canaan's land, "Let My people go!"

Thank You, Lord, for saving my soul.
Thank You, Lord for making me whole.
Thank You, Lord, for giving to me
Thy great salvation, so rich and free.

Blessings,
Don

Daily Praise Moment

March 17

Praising Our God Who Helps Us Work through the Hard Times

Jeremiah 33:3 (NKJV) says,
"Call to Me, and I will answer you, and show you great and mighty things, which you do not know."

Have you ever been stressed out, when you just didn't know what to do? I certainly have – several times. One time in particular stands out in my mind. It was during the spring of 1972. I was nearing the end of my year of teaching at Maryville College, a position I had taken on an interim basis. After sending out numerous resumes, one school called me, conducted a telephone interview and offered me a college teaching position, but to take that position would mean moving to Charleston, South Carolina.

Janet and I were proud parents of a beautiful little one-year-old boy. Moving away from doting grandparents would be hard.

Before moving to Maryville, Janet and I had worked with deaf children in Sunday school at First Baptist Church, Knoxville. And even though I was teaching sociology at the college level, working with deaf people as a career was consuming me.

One Sunday afternoon, Janet and I drove from Maryville to Fontana Dam. The drive was beautiful – a perfectly clear day. Vance was enjoying the ride and I hadn't made Janet car sick! Everything seemed to be perfect, except for one thing. That one thing was the way I felt inside my head. We pulled over at a rest stop, looking down on the beautiful river. I walked up the side of the mountain, sat down on a rock and just stared. Janet asked me what was wrong.

My reply – "I'm a quarter of a century old. One-third of my life is gone, and what have I accomplished?"

In reality, I had a beautiful wife who was perfect for me, a beautiful child, a master's degree, and was about to successfully complete my first full year of college teaching. But inside, I felt like a failure. In this time and place in my life, God began to give me comfort and direction.

I went back to see my old vocational rehabilitation counselor who had helped me when I was first released from the tuberculosis hospital. When I told him about my interest in working with deaf people, he got excited. He said that the Division of Vocational Rehabilitation was about to have a counselor vacancy. They were going to be looking for a person who knew American Sign Language who had a social sciences background. The person they were going to hire would provide vocational and personal adjustment counseling to teenagers who were deaf. He went on to say that if I was interested, he could get me an interview. I immediately said, "Yes, I'm very interested." He took me down the hall and introduced me to all of his work associates. He told them that I was "his client" and that I might be interested in "joining the team."

After my interview, I was offered the job, but the state was under a hiring freeze. I turned down the job in South Carolina; then, waited for the appointment to be approved. I joined the ranks of the unemployed for 10 weeks. Life was tight.

When the position was finally approved, my daily drive from Maryville to the Tennessee School for the Deaf was truly a time of worship and praise. God flooded my mind with Bible verses that I had learned as a child. Songs and choruses were on my lips as I drove my un-air-conditioned VW bug, singing at the top of my lungs! About a year later, a man who went to my church and worked for the telephone company said, "I meet you driving to work almost every day, and I don't think I've ever seen anyone who seems to be as happy as you do." And, he was right!

As I think about today's Scripture and the events that I've described, my musical mind hearing "Yes, Lord, Yes," by Lynn Keeseker:

I'll say yes, Lord, yes, to Your will and to Your way
I'll say yes, Lord, yes, I will trust You and obey
When the Spirit speaks to me, with my whole heart I'll agree
And my answer will be Yes, Lord, yes.

Blessings,
Don

Daily Praise Moment

March 18

Praising Our God Who Has Chosen Us to Be His People and Has Clothed Us with Kindness and Compassion

Colossians 3:12 -14 (NKJV) says:
Therefore, as the elect of God, holy and beloved, put on tender mercies, kindness, humility, meekness, longsuffering; bearing with one another, and forgiving one another, if anyone has a complaint against another; even as Christ forgave you, so you also must do. But above all these things put on love, which is the bond of perfection.

The church I grew up in, Corinth Missionary Baptist in Loudon, Tenn., always had Decoration Day on the fourth Sunday of May. Decorating began on Saturday morning. Then, on Decoration Day, we had morning worship, "dinner on the grounds" and gospel singing. It was the big event of the church. During my childhood, most the families either grew their own flowers or made them from crepe paper and paraffin. My mother and other ladies in our community spent hours making beautiful arrangements of flowers.

As folks began their decorating on Saturday morning, friendships were renewed with out-of-towners who came "home" each year. People talked about the impact that people buried in the cemetery had made on their lives.

One year as our family and many others gathered to do our decorating, my younger brother, Larry, who was about 7 at that time, began playing and running through the cemetery. When he became tired, he stopped and stood on the base of a grave marker. As he held onto the top of the tombstone, it gave way and fell over on him, trapping his leg. Fortunately, he wasn't seriously hurt. The weight of the stone could have killed or at least seriously injured him.

After this "near death" event, Larry went to Daddy and asked for a nickel to go to the grocery store next to church and buy a cup of ice cream. Daddy didn't have change, so he gave Larry a dollar. Money was very tight at that time. A dollar would buy four gallons of gas, so when Daddy gave the money, he was sure that he would have ninety-five cents in change when we got home.

Larry left us, walked to the store, bought ice cream and headed home. Our house was about a half mile from the church. When we arrived home, we found Larry enjoying his third cup of ice cream. Larry proudly showed Mom and Dad seven more cups of ice cream in the freezer. Instead of buying a nickel cup of ice cream as Daddy thought he would do, Larry had bought twenty cups of ice cream. His caring heart, though, led him to give ten cups of ice cream to Charlene, the little girl who lived next door.

I don't know if it was the "near death" experience or the fact that Larry had shared the ice cream with the neighbor child that led Daddy to laugh instead of frown. Either way, though, Larry got off the hook, enjoyed his ice cream, and made a memory that I've been enjoying for more than fifty years.

God loves us. To Him, those of us who know Him are holy and beloved. Thank God, He sees us through the blood of Jesus Christ. He wants us to put on tender mercies, kindness, humility and all the other traits mentioned in Colossians 3:12. He wants us to "share" our ice cream with others. And, He wants us to forgive others when things don't turn out the way we think they will. After all, life is about relationships, not about the change we think we'll get back.

As I think about today's Scripture and the scenario that I've described, my musical mind begins to hear Don Moen singing "Think About His Love," written by Walt Harrah:

Think about His love, think about His goodness
Think about His grace that's brought us through
For as high as the heavens above
So great is the measure of our Father's love
Great is the measure of our Father's love
So great is the measure of our Father's love

Blessings,
Don

Daily Praise Moment

March 19

Praising Our God Who Is ALWAYS with Us

Hebrews 13:5 (NKJV) says,
Let your conduct be without covetousness; be content with such things as you have. For He Himself has said, "I will never leave you nor forsake you.

God's will for us is that we be content in Him. Even in times when we feel alone, people who have a personal relationship with Christ are never alone.

We sometimes feel alone when things go wrong – family members pass; careers goes south; our health declines; friends move away, etc.

Yet, even in these tough times, God is still with us. As today's verse clearly states, the writer of Hebrews was inspired because the Lord said to Him (and to us), "I will never leave you nor forsake you."

In January of 2006, my dear Mother went home to be with the Lord. She was one of my major spiritual mentors. All my life I learned from her. The night of her death, I had the privilege of holding her in my arms and singing to her for the last 45 minutes of her life. I felt very blessed to have been able to be with her as she passed from my loving arms into the loving arms of our Savior.

Soon after Mom's death, my work life began to change markedly. Stress was intense as decisions were being made which dramatically impacted everyone involved in serving families whose very young children had disabilities. Trust levels were compromised. While I never doubted the Lord's presence, I often felt that I was alone. The stress continued to grow as time passed.

Then, about a year after Mom was "absent from the body, but present with the Lord," God spoke to me in a most unusual and wonderful way. I was at home one evening, going through my laptop computer bag. I was looking for something I needed when I discovered an envelope that was addressed to me, an envelope that I had never seen or opened.

I opened the envelope and found a notecard with a rose on the cover. Imprinted above the rose were these words: "I love you. . . ." Inside the card was a message penned by my precious Mom. I have no idea when she wrote it – her penmanship had suffered as she neared death, and this note was clearly written by my Mom's beautiful handwriting. It said, "Don, for the 10,000th time I've said 'I love you.' Now I'm saying it again. "Always, I will love you." "I don't want you to be sick. Hope you feel better soon. Your Mom"

Prior to Mom's death there were many times when Mom would say, "I went to Nashville with you yesterday." What she meant was that she had prayed for me throughout my trip. Then, a year after Mom's Heavenly home-going, I mysteriously found the unopened note telling me of her love.

Even more important, though, is the fact that the Lord Jesus Christ loves me. And He loves you, too. Because of His atoning sacrifice, my sin debt has been paid and I have a home in Heaven. When I leave this life, I'll arrive home in Heaven to be with Christ forever. And, I'll see Mom again, because she knew my Lord, too.

As I think of today's Scripture, my musical mind begins to hear one of the songs I sang to Mom just prior to her death. The song, "Lullaby," written by Don Francisco, has these beautiful lyrics:

Darkness covers all the land – sounds of day are gone;
But love is all around you now and will be 'till the dawn.
Stars shine on the window sill, moon shines through the trees;
Angels by your bed tonight – shine where no one sees.
So there's no need to be afraid all the whole night through
'Cause God has made a promise, child, that He'll take care of you.

Stars shine on the window sill, moon shines through the trees;
Angels by your bed tonight – shine where no one sees.
All that you've been dreaming of awaits you when you rise;
So with the peace that Jesus brings, close your sleepy eyes.

Blessings,
Don

Daily Praise Moment

March 20

Praising Our God Who Uses Believers as Salt to Season and Preserve

Matthew 5:13-14, (NKJV), says:
[13] *"You are the salt of the earth; but if the salt loses its flavor, how shall it be seasoned? It is then good for nothing but to be thrown out and trampled underfoot by men."*

This Scripture is God's way of telling us that believers have an important role to fulfill in His Kingdom. When we live out our purpose, God uses us to make a difference in the lives of others.

Salt is an interesting substance. It is truly amazing the difference in taste that comes from adding just a "pinch" of salt to some foods.

When I was in high school, my Dad bought a small "Mom and Pop" restaurant in Loudon. Dad had never worked in a restaurant, but he was desperate for a job, and the restaurant owner was equally desperate to retire. Our little restaurant, Country Joe's Café, was located across the street from Dr. Watkins' office.

Almost every Saturday, the parking spaces in front of Dr. Watkins' office were filled with "out of state" cars as people from several states would drive in to get a special medication that Dr. Watkins made to treat ulcers. Then, many of these "out of state folks" would come over to our little restaurant and eat things that had been off their "okay to eat" list for years. I'm certainly unlearned in medicine, but whatever Dr. Watkins made seemed to work! People were VERY happy to order liver and onions, gravy, and anything else they could think of. As soon as their food arrived, they would add salt to give it seasoning and flavor they longed to enjoy.

Salt is also a preservative. When I was a child, we had a Smokehouse. Inside the Smokehouse was a saltbox. When the weather got cold and hogs were butchered, the meat was packed in salt in the saltbox to preserve it. Salt kept it from spoiling.

God's Word says believers are the "salt of the earth." (Matthew 5a:13). Our role is to add a distinctly positive flavor to the lives of the folks with whom we associate. Further, He wants to use us to protect others from eternally missing the joys of Heaven.

The key, though, is that believers must remain true to our calling. If we get off mission, we don't really add that positive flavor. If we think that it is "all about us" and forget that our role is to season, then, instead of having a positive impact, we can undermine God's purpose for us and have a destructive impact on God's work.

Salt that becomes contaminated may be fine for melting ice on a parking lot, but it is not appropriate to use on food that we are about to eat. God wants His children to maintain pure lives so we can bring out the best in those with whom we have contact. He wants to use us to lead others to Him. As we lead others to Him, we are fulfilling our divine role of being His salt.

Salt also makes people thirsty. Remember what Jesus told the "woman at the well," recorded in John 4:14? He said: "…whoever drinks of the water that I shall give him will never thirst. But the water that I shall give him will become in him a fountain of water springing up into everlasting life." God wants to use us as His salt to make people thirsty for the "Fountain of Living Water," the Lord Jesus Christ Himself. After all, He is the ultimate "life preserver."

As I think of today's Scriptures, my musical mind begins hearing, "Satisfied," by Clara T. Williams, with music by Ralph E. Hudson:

All my life long I had panted for a draught from some cool spring,
That I hoped would quench the burning of the thirst I felt within.
Hallelujah! I have found Him, whom my soul so long has craved!
Jesus satisfies my longings; through His blood I now am saved.

Well of water, ever springing, Bread of life, so rich and free,
Untold wealth that never faileth, my Redeemer is to me.
Hallelujah! I have found Him, whom my soul so long has craved!
Jesus satisfies my longings; through His blood I now am saved.

Blessings,
Don

Daily Praise Moment

March 21

Praising Our God Who Uses Us to Be His Hands, Serving Others

Matthew 25: 34-40 (NKJV) records Jesus' words to His disciples and to us:
"Then the King will say to those on His right hand, Come, you blessed of My Father, inherit the kingdom prepared for you from the foundation of the world:
35 for I was hungry and you gave Me food; I was thirsty and you gave Me drink; I was a stranger and you took Me in;
36 I was naked and you clothed Me; I was sick and you visited Me; I was in prison and you came to Me.

37 Then the righteous will answer Him, saying, Lord, when did we see You hungry and feed You, or thirsty and give You drink?
38 When did we see You a stranger and take You in, or naked and clothe You?
39 Or when did we see You sick, or in prison, and come to You?
40 And the King will answer and say to them, Assuredly, I say to you, inasmuch as you did it to one of the least of these My brethren, you did it to Me."

I've heard Bible scholars say that the word "believe" means more than just giving mental assent. The word implies action. It is something that we do! Having a "**believe – to do"** mindset means taking risks, and sometimes the risks we take cause concern.

A few years ago, Janet and I were having a meal with a couple from North Carolina. The husband was the minister of music in a church, and his wife was an elementary school guidance counselor. She began telling us about how she was trying to build rapport with the students in her new school. She went to each classroom and told the children that they didn't have to have a crisis to be able to come and talk with her – they could come to see her to share good news, too.

One day a little kindergarten girl came running into her office very excited, smiling ear-to-ear. She jumped into our friend's arms and said, "Mrs. Neal, Mrs. Neal, I have good news." Our friend said, "That's great! Tell me your good news." The little girl gave Mrs. Neal another hug and said, "My Daddy is coming to school to get me. I get to go home early!"

Mrs. Neal smiled and said, "I'm curious. Tell me why you're getting to go home early?" The little girl smiled, gave Mrs. Neal another hug and said, "I've got lice!"

God wants us involved in our communities, being salt and light to a lost, hurting world. As we faithfully serve others, those we are serving see our Savior and want Him living in their hearts, too.

As I think of today's Scripture and the incident I've described, my musical mind begins to hear this song, written by Eva B. Lloyd, and sung to a traditional American melody, *The Sacred Harp, 1844*:

Come, all Christians, be committed to the service of the Lord;
Make your lives for him more fitted, tune your hearts with one accord.
Come into His courts with gladness, each his sacred vows renew, turn away from sin and sadness, be transformed with life anew.

Of your time and talents give ye, they are gifts from God above;
To be used by Christians freely to proclaim His wondrous love.
Come again to serve the Savior, tithes and off'rings with you bring.
In your work, with Him find favor, and with joy His praises sing.

God's command to love each other is required of every man;
Showing mercy to a brother mirrors His redemptive plan.
In compassion He has given of His love that is divine;
On the cross sins were forgiven; joy and peace are fully thine.

Come in praise and adoration, all who in Christ's name believe;
Worship Him with consecration, grace and love you will receive.
For His grace give Him the glory, for the Spirit and the Word,
And repeat the gospel story till all men His name have heard.

Blessings,
Don

Daily Praise Moment

March 22

Praising Our God Who Is Our Security

Psalm 55:22 (NASB), says:
Cast your burden upon the LORD and He will sustain you; He will never allow the righteous to be shaken.

Hebrews 13:6 (NASB), says:
The Lord is my helper, I will not be afraid. What will man do to me?

Believing in Jesus Christ does not mean that we are automatically shielded from life. But it does mean that we are never forsaken.

When I was a child, Roy Rogers, Lash LaRue, The Cisco Kid, Gene Autry and others were the good guys and the good guys always won.

Satan uses fear to control us. He wants to hamper our personal walk with the Savior. About ten years ago, a young man in my Sunday school class gave me an acrostic for the word, FEAR -- **F**alse **E**xpectations **A**ppearing **R**eal.

Remember the time when Jesus asked Simon Peter who people were saying He was? Peter gave Jesus a list of people that some were saying Jesus might be. Then, Jesus asked Peter the important question, "Who do you say that I am?" Peter said, "You are the Christ, the Son of the Living God."

What Jesus said next really intrigues me (see Matthew 16:18 (KJV))
"And I say also unto thee, that thou art Peter, and upon this rock I will build my church; and the gates of hell shall not prevail against it."

Have you ever seen soldiers carrying gates into battle? I doubt it. Gates are usually erected to guard a city. Since gates don't normally go into battle, I believe that God wants us to realize that our charge is to take the battle to the "gates of hell." As believers, our role is to "set the captives free." Matthew 16:18 clearly says that the gates won't prevail!

As I think about today's Scriptures, my musical mind begins to hear "Be Ye Glad," by M. K. Blanchard (Please give special attention to the lyrics that are bolded.)

In these days of confused situations. In these nights of a restless remorse, when the heart and the soul of the nation, lay wounded and cold as a corpse. From the grave of the innocent Adam, comes a song bringing joy to the sad. Oh your cry has been heard and the ransom, has been paid up in full, Be Ye Glad. Oh, Be Ye Glad, Oh, Be Ye Glad, Every debt that you ever had has been paid up in full by the grace of the Lord, Be Ye Glad, Be Ye Glad, Be Ye Glad.

From the dungeon a rumor is stirring, though you've heard it again and again. Ah, but this time the cell keys are turning, and outside there are faces of friends. And though your body lay weary from wasting, and your eyes show the sorrow they've had, Oh the love that your heart is now tasting has opened the gate, Be Ye Glad. Oh, Be Ye Glad, Oh, Be Ye Glad, every debt that you ever had has been paid up in full by the grace of the Lord, Be Ye Glad, Be Ye Glad, Be Ye Glad.

So be like lights on the rim of the water, giving hope in a storm sea of night. Be a refuge amidst the slaughter for these fugitives in their flight. For you are timeless and part of a puzzle. You are winsome and young as a lad. And there is no disease or no struggle, that can pull you from God, Be Ye Glad. Oh, Be Ye Glad, Oh, Be Ye Glad, Every debt that you ever had has been paid up in full by the grace of the Lord, Be Ye Glad, Be Ye Glad, Be Ye Glad. Oh, Be Ye Glad, Oh, Be Ye Glad, Every debt that you ever had Has been paid up in full by the grace of the Lord, Be Ye Glad, Be Ye Glad, Be Ye Glad.

Blessings,
Don

Daily Praise Moment

March 23

Praising Our God Who Wants Us to Leave a Godly Heritage for Others to Follow

Psalm 78:5-7 (NKJV) says:
5 *For He established a testimony in Jacob, And appointed a law in*
Israel, Which He commanded our fathers, That they should make them
known to their children; 6 *That the generation to come might know*
them, The children who would be born, That they may arise and
declare them to their children, 7 *That they may set their hope in God,*
And not forget the works of God, But keep His commandments.

I grew up in a time when there were four basic location options for children: 1) at home, 2) at school, 3) with family or friends of the family, or 4) at church. The only events that superseded church were major disasters, funerals or other tragedies. No school or sports activities were ever planned on Sunday mornings. The high school band or chorus might have a Sunday afternoon concert, but these never conflicted with church. The only school activities I can remember ever happening on Sunday evenings were baccalaureate services for high school seniors, and these were usually conducted by ordained ministers.

Our culture has markedly changed since I was a child, and as the emphasis on corporate worship has declined, so have cultural standards. Vocabulary that was limited to certain places is now common on TV, in restaurants, and at sports events. As moral standards have declined, so have the values associated with human life. At my country church, the church bell rang each Sunday morning and Sunday evening, signifying time for worship. When the same bell rang during the day on a week day, we all knew that it meant that someone had passed away. The bell sound that was bright and cheerful on Sundays was sad and sobering during the week!

My dad was the song leader in our church. Our choir often sang for funerals, and we grieved with families during their times of loss -- the level of support for families was sincere.

The biggest need that believers have, apart from a strong personal relationship with Christ, is to have strong, personal relationships with other people. After all, whether we want to admit it or not, all of us are terminally ill. There will be a time when the bell tolls for us. God wants believers to leave a legacy so others will follow Him.

As I think on today's Scripture, my musical mind begins to hear "Find Us Faithful," written by Jon Mohr:

We're pilgrims on the journey of the narrow road, and those who've gone before us line the way, cheering on the faithful, encouraging the weary, their lives a stirring testament to God's sustaining grace.

Surrounded by so great a cloud of witnesses, let us run the race not only for the prize, but as those who've gone before us, let us leave to those behind us the heritage of faithfulness passed on through godly lives.

Oh may all who come behind us find us faithful. May the fire of our devotion light their way. May the footprints that we leave lead them to believe, and the lives we live inspire them to obey. Oh may all who come behind us find us faithful.

After all our hopes and dreams have come and gone, and our children sift through all we've left behind, may the clues that they discover and the memories they uncover become the light that leads them to the road we each must find.

Oh may all who come behind us find us faithful. May the fire of our devotion light their way. May the footprints that we leave lead them to believe and the lives we live inspire them to obey. Oh may all who come behind us find us faithful.

Blessings,
Don

Daily Praise Moment

March 24

Praising Our God, Our Friend Who Teaches Us How to Be a Friend

Ecclesiastes 4:9-10 (NKJV), says:
9 Two are better than one, Because they have a good reward for their labor. 10 For if they fall, one will lift up his companion. But woe to him who is alone when he falls, For he has no one to help him up.

Proverbs 17:17 (NKJV), has these words:
17 A friend loves at all times, And a brother is born for adversity.

The older I become, the more I value friends. Years can pass but when friends cross paths, we're back to where we were years ago.

Some time ago, I received a phone call from a childhood friend and neighbor that I had not seen in years. Betty called to let me know that her dad was declining in health and that if I had a desire to see him and have conversation with him, I'd need to do it soon. Shortly thereafter, I ran into another childhood friend, Terry Bright. The two of us went to see Betty's parents, Joe and Sally Caldwell. Joe was pastor of our church when Terry and I were growing up. All of us were neighbors, too, living a stone's throw from each other. Terry and I had a wonderful visit with Joe and Sally. Both of us were able to tell them how much their lives had positively influenced us.

After our visit I called Joe's son, Boyd. We hadn't seen each other for at least 35 years, but within one minute, we were getting caught up. It was great! I always looked up to Boyd when I was a child. He was always full of energy, and if something was happening, Boyd was in the middle of it. When a neighbor set up a saw mill, Boyd led a group of us to the sawmill to get enough slab lumber to build two cabins on the land beside the creek that ran behind his home and in front of my home. One night as we camped in our cabins, a huge thunderstorm "came up" and my Mom came with a flashlight and got us all into our homes just before the creek overran its banks!

I remember spending the night at Boyd's home once and going with him to visit his uncle who had just bought about twenty ponies. They were in the field and we caught two of them and went for rides.

We didn't have saddles, and my pony succeeded in scraping me off his back, rubbing me against the side of the barn. When I fell off, the pony stepped on my back and left his hoof print on my T-shirt. I threw it away so my Mom wouldn't know what had happened.

Boyd was always the first to try anything dangerous. Once we managed to roll a big truck tire to the top of the hill behind our homes. Boyd "talked up the notion" of someone getting inside the tire and riding it down the steep hill. He even volunteered to be the first rider. Reluctantly, we all agreed. Boyd got in the tire and we sent him careening down the hill. The tire hit the dry creek bed, and went airborne. Miraculously, Boyd survived. The "death defying truck tire ride" only made one trip. No one else risked the ride.

Friends are wonderful. The very best friend we can ever have is Jesus Christ. He is the Friend who never leaves us nor forsakes us. I hope you know Him. If you're unsure, please contact me and I'll introduce you to Him.

As I think of today's Scripture verses and the scenes I've described, my musical mind begins to hear this old hymn, written by James G. Small in 1863:

I've found a Friend, O such a friend! He loved me ere I knew Him. He drew me with the cords of love, and thus He bound me to Him. And round my heart still closely twine those ties which naught can sever, for I am His, and He is mine, forever and forever.

I've found a Friend, O such a friend! He bled, He died to save me And not alone the gift of life, but His own Self He gave me! Naught that I have mine own I call, I'll hold it for the Giver. My heart, my strength, my life, my all are His, and His forever.

I've found a Friend, O such a friend! So kind and true and tender. So wise a Counselor and Guide, so mighty a Defender! From Him who loves me now so well what power my soul can sever? Shall life or death, shall earth or hell? No! I am His forever.

Blessings,
Don

Daily Praise Moment

March 25

Praising Our God Who Is the Light of the World

John 8:12 (NKJV) says:
[12] *Then Jesus spoke to them again, saying, "I am the light of the world. He who follows Me shall not walk in darkness, but have the light of life."*

In Matthew 5:14 (NKJV), Jesus told His disciples:
[14] *"You are the light of the world. A city that is set on a hill cannot be hidden.* [15] *Nor do they light a lamp and put it under a basket, but on a lampstand, and it gives light to all who are in the house.* [16] *Let your light so shine before men, that they may see your good works and glorify your Father in heaven."*

Each Saturday morning at 7 a.m., a group of us meets together to pray for the work of The Gideons International, a ministry that is sharing the gospel in 200 countries. One Saturday morning about six years ago, Max Willocks, who is involved in international missions work, came with his brother-in-law, Gayle Ferguson, to our Gideons prayer time. Max was on the verge of being 88 years old at that time. What he shared with us really challenged my heart. Some of the comments he made were:

"The program of Christianity – are we really doing it? There are still 3,800 people groups who haven't heard. Does Jesus think that what we're doing is enough?"

"When we go to Heaven, will He say to us, 'Well done' or not?"

"Is building more buildings better? There were NO church buildings during the first 300 years of the Christian church!"

"It bothers me that we spend so much to reach some people for Christ, but don't reach many."

"I've done traditional missions for more than 50 years. I've seen 400 people come to Christ in one night, but is this really the New Testament way?"

Max went on to explain that his whole mental model of ministry has changed to a "home church" model in the last ten years. In 2003, he and a small team went to Kenya to do a mission project with local Kenyan pastors. The pastors thought Max's team was coming to build buildings for them. Their intention, though, was to give training on how to establish "home churches." One of the Kenyan pastors was very opposed initially; however, since that time, this particular pastor has started more than 6,500 home churches. Today, "in Kenya, there are over 70,000 new home churches starting each month."

Max then asked us this question: "Are we attending church, or are we attending a church building?" "Are we coming to hear our minister 'kick our shins,' then, leaving and doing nothing?"

Finally, Max made a summary colloquial statement regarding the state of church work in the United States today. What he said was, "We're not just 'sot' in our ways. We're buried in our ways." Again, this elderly gentleman challenged my heart.

As I think of today's Scriptures and Max's comments, my musical mind begins to hear "Carry the Light," by Twila Paris:

In this world of darkness, we are given light. Hope for all the dying. How will they know? How will they know that Jesus loves them and He died to save them? Carry the Light. Carry the Light. Go and tell the children they are precious in His sight. Carry the Light. Carry the Light. Go and preach the gospel 'til there is no more night. In the name of Jesus Christ, carry the Light.

Count them by the millions, blinded slaves to sin. Inside they are dying. How will they know? How will they know that Jesus loves them and His heart is breaking? Go ye into all the world. Go ye into all the world. And carry the Light the Light. Carry the Light.

Blessings,
Don

Daily Praise Moment

March 26

Praising Our God Who Leads Us in Paths of Righteousness

Psalm 23:1, 3 (NKJV), says:
"The Lord is my shepherd; I shall not want... [3] He restores my soul; ***He leads me in the paths of righteousness for His name's sake."***

2 Chronicles 7:14 (NKJV) says:
"If My people who are called by My name will humble themselves, and pray and seek My face, and turn from their wicked ways, then I will hear from heaven, and will forgive their sin and heal their land."

All of us are tempted to violate God's purpose and plan for our lives and we make mistakes and sin. However, in our "heart of hearts," true believers want to walk in the "Paths of Righteousness" for God's name's sake. We don't want our choices and behavior to make unbelievers look down on our Savior. God wants to break the bondage that believers are under when we are not walking with Him. He wants to set us free. He wants revival and renewal to be evident in our hearts and lives, but we have some serious renewal to go through in order to experience God's best.

I recently listened to a challenging sermon by Dr. Derek Prince who passed away a number of years ago, but the messages he gave are still very challenging. He pointed out that God requires four things of His believers before He will provide the three answers that are promised in 2 Chronicles 7:14.

Believers are to "humble themselves." God doesn't do the humbling. He tells us to choose to "humble ourselves." Throughout the Bible, many people humbled themselves by fasting. God may not lead us to fast, but He certainly wants us to stop thinking that everything is all about us. It isn't. It's all about Him!

Believers are to "pray." God wants us to remember that prayer is NOT monologue with God. Prayer is dialog with God. We dialogue with God by hearing His voice when He speaks to us through His Word, and when His Holy Spirit reveals Bible truth to us.

Believers are told to "seek God's face." We do this by faithfully reading God's Word and applying His Word to our hearts. He wants us to seek God's face above all our other desires in life.

Believers are to "turn from our wicked ways." This means more than just feeling sorry when we "get caught." Turning from our wicked ways involves doing right by God, regardless of the cost that might come.

As we do these four things, God promises us that He will take the following three "conditional actions" on our behalf:

God will "hear from Heaven." He isn't just a static God who rarely gets involved. He hears our calls and cries for help and intervenes.

God will "forgive our sin." God genuinely separates us from our sinful past. As Psalm 103:12 says, He takes our sins as far away from us as East is from the West.

God will "heal our land." The healing of our land will come when we, as God's people, do the four tasks that God has assigned us to do.

Revival depends on Christians yielding to Almighty God.

As I reflect on today's Scriptures, my spiritual mind begins to hear "Search Me, O God," written by J. Edwin Orr in 1936, with text based on Psalm 139:23.

Search me, O God, and know my heart today. Try me, O Savior, know my thoughts, I pray; see if there be some wicked way in me. Cleanse me from every sin, and set me free.

I praise Thee, Lord, for cleansing me from sin; fulfill Thy word and make me pure within; fill me with fire, where once I burned with shame; grant my desire to magnify Thy name.

Blessings,
Don

Daily Praise Moment

March 27

Praising Our God Who Gives Us Joy, Even When We Face Hard Times

Psalm 30:11-12 (NIV), says:
11 *You turned my wailing into dancing;*
You removed my sackcloth and clothed me with joy,
12 *that my heart may sing your praises and not be silent.*
LORD my God, I will praise you forever.

This psalm was apparently written by David after he had come through a near-death experience. Near-death experiences weren't new for David. Throughout his life, he faced challenges that could have been fatal.

As a young teenager, David tended his father's sheep. 1 Samuel 17:34-36 records David's testimony regarding how he faced both a mountain lion and a bear that came to attack his father's sheep. Rather than shudder in fear, David pursued the lion and the bear, rescued the sheep and killed both the lion and the bear.

Later, when David was obeying his father and taking food to his brothers who were in the army, David heard Goliath challenging the entire Israelite army. David interpreted Goliath's taunting as an affront to God Almighty.

Rather than see their baby brother's offer to face Goliath as a noble act, David's brothers belittled him. David's brothers and the other Israelite soldiers were looking at Goliath's size and seeing him as an enemy too large to defeat. They were thinking, "Look how much bigger Goliath is than David." David was thinking, "Look how much bigger God is than Goliath." While the soldiers saw Goliath as too big to hit, David saw Goliath as too big to miss!

Later in life, David faced the attacks of King Saul. On at least two occasions, David had the option of taking Saul's life. Certainly, that would have ended Saul's attacks, but David knew that taking matters into his own hands without God's leading him to do so was wrong. David listened to God and God took care of the problem for him.

David had gotten to know God in the desert, during times when the only one near him was God.

It is very important for us to get to know God well. Why? Because sooner or later, like David, we'll all face a Goliath in our lives. Maybe our Goliath will be sickness. Maybe it will be job loss, or a relationship gone wrong. Whatever the challenge, when we truly know God, we can rely on Him to see us through.

As I review today's Scripture and think about the challenges David faced, my musical mind begins to hear my brother, Bill, sing Squire Parsons' song, "I Sing Because."

I've been singing about my Lord for many years. I've sung when I've been happy, I've sung when I've had fears, and some folks may even question if it's all been just for show, well the reason that I'm singing, I want the World to know.

I sing because there is an empty grave, I sing because there is a power that saves, I sing because His grace is real to me, I sing because I am not alone, I sing because someday I'm going home, Where I shall sing thru all eternity.

I've sung to those walking thru the fiery trial, and I've watched their saddened faces turn into happy smiles, and I've bowed my head and whispered, "Lord, Please do the same for me," and I'm glad that I can tell you, He's always given victory.

I sing because there is an empty grave, I sing because there is a power that saves, I sing because His grace is real to me, I sing because I am not alone, I sing because someday I'm going home, Where I shall sing thru all eternity.

Blessings,
Don

Daily Praise Moment

March 28

Praising Our God Who Is Always Trustworthy

1 Timothy 4:9-10 (NKJV) says:
[9] This is a faithful saying and worthy of all acceptance. [10] For to this end we both labor and suffer reproach, because we trust in the living God, who is the Savior of all men, especially of those who believe.

In the summer of 1967, I was a student at Hiwassee College. I was taking a swimming class to fulfill my physical education requirement. Sounds like fun, doesn't it! It was, except that the class met at 8 a.m., and the outside pool was spring-fed. The water probably felt good on a hot afternoon, but not at 8 a.m.

The teacher of the class was Nick Menacof, Hiwassee's athletic director. On the first day of class, Coach Menacof had us jump from the diving board, spread our legs in a scissors pattern and extend our arms horizontally. When we made contact with the water, we were to scissor our legs similar to a flutter kick, and bring our arms to a closed position. When we did this successfully, our heads did not go under. The first day of class, everyone successfully executed the command except for one young man. As he closed his arms in front of him, he sank to the bottom of the pool. Coach Menacof used his rescue hook to retrieve him. Once he was out of the pool, the young man was fine. He never seemed fearful, but each time he jumped, he sank. And, each time he sank, Coach Menacof retrieved him.

We went through various other training exercises in the class, but each day, we started with the same task, and each day this young man was pulled out of the water by the teacher.

As I think of today's Scriptures, I'm reminded that even when we don't accomplish the task that we're trying to do, our God is faithful. He rescues us.

Remember Psalm 23:4, which says:
"Yea, though I walk through the valley of the shadow of death, I will fear no evil: for thou art with me; thy rod and thy staff they comfort me."

Many have thought that this verse refers to the correction that God gives us. Certainly, God does correct us. After all, He does have our best interests in His heart. Rather than just correction, though, I believe that a truer interpretation is that God's rod and staff comfort and protect us from other harms. Just as Coach Menacof pulled the young man from the water, God pulls us out of dangerous situations, too. As He is saving us, He wants us to learn from the "teachable moments" that we face.

As I think of today's Scripture verses and the scenes that I've described, my musical mind begins to hear "Great Is Thy Faithfulness," written by Thomas Chisholm (words) and William M. Runyan (music) in 1923:

Great is thy faithfulness, O God my Father; there is no shadow of turning with Thee;Thou changest not, Thy compassions, they fail not; as Thou hast been Thou forever will be. Great is Thy faithfulness! Great is Thy faithfulness! Morning by morning new mercies I see; all I have needed Thy hand hath provided; great is Thy faithfulness, Lord, unto me!

Summer and winter and springtime and harvest, sun, moon and stars in their courses above join with all nature in manifold witness To Thy great faithfulness, mercy and love. Great is Thy faithfulness! Great is Thy faithfulness! Morning by morning new mercies I see; all I have needed Thy hand hath provided; great is Thy faithfulness, Lord, unto me!

Pardon for sin and a peace that endureth, Thine own dear presence to cheer and to guide; strength for today and bright hope for tomorrow, Blessings all mine, with ten thousand beside! Great is thy faithfulness! Great is thy faithfulness! Morning by morning new mercies I see; all I have needed thy hand hath provided; great is thy faithfulness, Lord, unto me!

Blessings,
Don

Daily Praise Moment

March 29

Praising Our God Who Saves Us and Changes Our Perspective

Phil. 2: 5-8 (NASB) says,
[5] *Let this mind be in you which was also in Christ Jesus,* [6] *who, being in the form of God, did not consider it robbery to be equal with God,*
[7] *but made Himself of no reputation, taking the form of a bondservant, and coming in the likeness of men.* [8] *And being found in appearance as a man, He humbled Himself and became obedient to the point of death, even the death of the cross.*

Romans 12:2 (NKJV) says:
[2] *And do not be conformed to this world, but be transformed by the renewing of your mind, that you may prove what is that good and acceptable and perfect will of God.*

Everyone has a perspective. Our perspectives can change, too, based on the view we have of the situations and circumstances we are facing.

About ten years ago, I was walking in my neighborhood when I noticed that one of my neighbors had a dune buggy with a huge fan mounted to the back of it, sitting on a trailer in his driveway. Later, when I saw him outside in his yard, I stopped, struck up a conversation, and learned that the dune buggy was really a powered parachute plane. My neighbor asked me if I'd like to go for a ride, and I said, "YES."

A few days later, we took his powered parachute to a remote location, fired it up and took a ride. We were up approximately 300 – 600 feet, flying at about 25-30 mph. After about 30 minutes in the air, we flew over my home. I live near Asbury Place assisted living and retirement community. I've lived near Asbury for many years, and I've visited people who live there; however, I had forgotten that Asbury's assisted living facility is pentagon shaped. From the air, this was easy to see, but from the ground, it was not obvious to me. It is easy for us to reach wrong conclusions in life if we're seeing things from the wrong perspective.

God wants to change our hearts and our lives. When we meet Christ and allow Him to be Lord (Boss, Ruler) of our lives, His Holy Spirit empowers us to live a very different life. God wants us to see ourselves from His perspective -- we are His New Creations. God says that we are "*more than conquerors through Him who loved us*," and that "*nothing can separate us from God's love which is in Christ Jesus, our Lord*" (Romans 8:37-39).

As I think of these Scriptures, my musical mind begins to hear Kindred Hearts, a ladies trio from our church, sing "I've Been Changed," by Mosie Lister.

Well, I've been to the river, I've been baptized. I've been washed in the blood of the Lamb. I've been changed from the creature that once I was and redeemed is now my name. I've been changed, I'm new born now. All my life has been rearranged. What a difference it made when the Lord came and stayed in my heart, Oh, yes, I've been changed.

Though my sins were as scarlet, they're white as snow. I was bound, but today I am free. I was lost in the darkness, but now am found. I was blind, but now I see. I've been changed, I'm newborn now. All my life has been rearranged. What a difference it made when the Lord came and stayed in my heart, Oh, yes, I've been changed.

Like the poor Hebrew children, I wandered long in a bare desert land to and fro. But I've crossed over Jordan to Canaan's land where the milk and honey flow.

When at last in His presence, I stand above. He will wipe all the tears from my eyes. And I'll thank Him for giving a wretch like me Lasting Hope beyond the skies. I've been changed, I'm newborn now. All my life has been rearranged. What a difference it made when the Lord came and stayed in my heart, Oh, yes, I've been changed.

Blessings,
Don

Daily Praise Moment

March 30

Praising Our God Who Guides Us in Our Interchanges with Others

Proverbs 21:23 (NKJV) says:
Whoever guards his mouth and tongue keeps his soul from troubles.

1 Peter 4:11 (NKJV) says:
If anyone speaks, let him speak as the oracles of God. If anyone ministers, let him do it as with the ability which God supplies, that in all things God may be glorified through Jesus Christ, to whom belong the glory and the dominion forever and ever. Amen.

Proverbs 15:4 (NKJV) says:
A wholesome tongue is a tree of life, but perverseness in it breaks the spirit.

When I was a child, I often heard people say, "Sticks and stones may break my bones, but words will never hurt me." The message was, "let critical comments roll off your back." But word DO hurt us. We can all engage our tongues before we engage our brains. We can go from cool to red hot in a flash.

God wants to use us to build His Kingdom, but we can damage people's opinion of God simply by the way we respond to them.

When I was a student at Hiwassee College in the 1960s, our social psychology teacher explained how easy it is to make wrong decisions based on how we interpret information coming in our direction. After class, some of us met and decided to test out the teacher's information by doing an experiment.

Over lunch we concocted our plan. Not long thereafter, one of the girls in our class came in to get lunch. While she was waiting, one of the guys walked over to her, gave her an inquiring look and asked, "Are you okay today?" She responded with, "Yes, I'm fine." After she got her food and sat down to eat, the second guy walked over to her and said, "Are you feeling okay?" She said, "Yes, I'm alright. Why did you ask?" He said, "Oh, I don't know. I was just wondering if you felt okay; that's all." Soon thereafter, the third guy walked over, and with a very concerned look on his face, asked, "Are you alright?" To this, she responded, "I don't feel well. I'm going home. I think I'm coming down with something!"

We weren't being good friends to do this experiment on a "friend," but our "experiment" certainly drove home the point that we are all susceptible to being influenced by others.

God wants us to make wise decisions and behave in the situations we face by aligning our lives with His Word. As we do, He gives us divine guidance to respond appropriately. After all, as Hebrews 4:12 says, His Word is "*sharper than a two-edged sword.*"

As I think of today's Scriptures and the situations I've described, my musical mind begins to hear the Dwight Liles and Niles Borop song, "His Word Will Stand:"

Some say its myth and legend, one more book upon the shelf, but the message it contains cannot be stilled. For God who wrote its pages will not let it pass away; not one syllable will linger unfulfilled.

His Word will stand, His Word will stand, though stars should fall and mountains turn to sand. Though no man believes Him, still God will be true. His promise is sure, His love will endure, and forever His Word will stand.

Don't listen to the voices of a world caught up in fear, for the Word of God proclaims the victory. He gives His children courage to confront the gates of Hell with the Sword that conquers every enemy.

His Word will stand, His Word will stand, though stars should fall and mountains turn to sand. Though no man believes Him, still God will be true. His promise is sure, His love will endure, And forever His Word will stand. And forever His Word will stand. His Word will stand.

Blessings,
Don

Daily Praise Moment

March 31

Praising Our God Whose Word and Holy Spirit Guide Our Prayers

James 5:17-18 (NKJV) says:
[17] Elijah was a man with a nature like ours, and he prayed earnestly that it would not rain; and it did not rain on the land for three years and six months. [18] And he prayed again, and the heaven gave rain, and the earth produced its fruit.

My heart has been deeply touched by sermons on prayer by Dr. Derek Prince. One of the major lessons I'm learning is that God has given believers the responsibility for praying and impacting the world through our prayers. As we study God's Word, it is easy for us to assign attributes to Bible characters that make them different from us. When we do, we often miss seeing the fullness of what God is wanting us to learn.

One of the first truths to notice in the verses presented above is that Elijah is defined by God as a person "with a nature like ours." He was an "ordinary" guy, but the big difference was that he had an "extraordinary" prayer relationship with God.

The Jewish nation had turned its back on God, and Elijah prayed earnestly that it would not rain. He wanted physical hardships to convince the Jewish people that they, apart from God, were unable to satisfy basic needs. Later, when the Jewish people turned back to God, Elijah, under the influence and leadership of the Holy Spirit, prayed again, asking God to send rain and the drought was broken.

Exodus 19:3-6 (NKJV) says:
[3] "And Moses went up to God, and the Lord called to him from the mountain, saying, "Thus you shall say to the house of Jacob, and tell the children of Israel: [4] 'You have seen what I did to the Egyptians, and how I bore you on eagles' wings and brought you to Myself. [5] Now therefore, if you will indeed obey My voice and keep My covenant, then you shall be a special treasure to Me above all people; for all the earth is Mine. [6] And you shall be to Me a kingdom of priests and a holy nation.' These are the words which you shall speak to the children of Israel."

In Revelation 1:6 (NASV), Jesus is talking to believers, telling John to write these words:
". . . He has made us TO BE a kingdom, priests to His God and Father — to Him BE the glory and the dominion forever and ever. Amen."

What God is telling us through His Word is that we believers are a Kingdom of Priests to God. We have responsibility for fulfilling the priestly role that the priests fulfilled during Biblical times. We are to enter the throne room of Heaven and commune with the Heavenly Father. The good news is that Jesus is our Advocate in Heaven, pleading our case for us. Further, the Holy Spirit of God is living inside us believers, leading us to pray prayers that align with God's will.

In our culture, it is easy for us to play the "name and blame" game, attributing all of our hardships and failures on other people. The people we tend to blame most often are those in leadership roles.

As God's Kingdom of Priests, responsibility for where we are rests upon us.

To quote Dr. Prince, "God has made us a kingdom of Priests – Our responsibility is to rule by prayer. This world is not really ruled by presidents, kings and dictators. Those who really rule are those who know how to pray."

As I think on today's Scripture verses, my musical mind begins to hear "I Miss My Time with You," written to one of my musical heroes, Larnelle Harris:

There He was just waiting in our old familiar place,
An empty spot beside Him where once I used to wait
To be filled with strength and wisdom for the battles of the day.
I would've passed Him by again but I clearly heard Him say:

"I miss My time with you. Those moments together.
I need to be with you each day and it hurts Me when you say you're too busy, busy trying to serve Me but how can you serve Me when your spirit's empty? There's a longing in My heart wanting more than just a part of you It's true. I miss My time with you."

What will I have to offer? How can I truly care? My efforts have no meaning when Your presence isn't there. But You'll provide the power if I take time to pray, So I'll stay right here beside You And You'll never have to say:

"I miss My time with you. Those moments together. I need to be with you each day and it hurts Me when you say you're too busy, busy trying to serve Me, but how can you serve Me when your spirit's empty? There's a longing in My heart wanting more than just a part of you. It's true. I miss My time with you."

Blessings,
Don

Lessons to Learn, Ideas to Implement, Challenges to Explore

86495208R00104

Made in the USA
Columbia, SC
12 January 2018